RECEIV

HOLY S

A 70-day Journey through the Scriptures

RECEIVE THE

HOLY SPIRIT

DAN WILT

Unless otherwise noted, Scripture quotations are taken from the Holy Bible, New International Version®, NIV® Copyright © 1973, 1978, 1984, 2011 by Biblica, Inc.™ Used by permission of Zondervan. All rights reserved worldwide. www.zondervan.com The "NIV" and "New International Version" are trademarks registered in the United States Patent and Trademark Office by Biblica, Inc.™ All rights reserved worldwide.

Scripture quotations marked ESV are from The Holy Bible, English Standard Version®, copyright © 2001 by Crossway, a publishing ministry of Good News Publishers. Used by permission. All rights reserved.

Printed in the United States of America

Cover and page design by Strange Last Name
Page layout by PerfecType, Nashville, Tennessee

Wilt, Dan
   Receive the Holy Spirit : a 70-day journey through the scriptures / Dan Wilt. – Franklin, Tennessee : Seedbed Publishing, ©2022.

       pages ; cm.

       Includes bibliographical references.
       ISBN: 9781628249262 (paperback)
       ISBN: 9781628249279 (mobi)
       ISBN: 9781628249286 (epub)
       ISBN: 9781628249293 (pdf)
       OCLC: 1298231291

       1. Holy Spirit--Biblical teaching. 2. Holy Spirit--Meditations.
       3. Fruit of the Spirit.   I. Title.

BT121.3.W54 2022   231.3   2022933110

SEEDBED PUBLISHING
Franklin, Tennessee
seedbed.com

To my family in the Vineyard Movement:
thank you for teaching me what it means to live
a life that is responsive to the Holy Spirit.

CONTENTS

AN INVITATION TO AWAKENING

This resource comes with an invitation.

The invitation is as simple as it is comprehensive. It is not an invitation to commit your life to this or that cause or to join an organization or to purchase another book. The invitation is this: to wake up to the life you always hoped was possible and the reason you were put on planet Earth.

It begins with following Jesus Christ. In case you are unaware, Jesus was born in the first century BCE into a poor family from Nazareth, a small village located in what is modern-day Israel. While his birth was associated with extraordinary phenomena, we know little about his childhood. At approximately thirty years of age, Jesus began a public mission of preaching, teaching, and healing throughout the region known as Galilee. His mission was characterized by miraculous signs and wonders; extravagant care of the poor and marginalized; and multiple unconventional claims about his own identity and purpose. In short, he claimed to be the incarnate Son of God with the mission and power to save people from sin, deliver them from death, and bring them into the now and eternal kingdom of God—on earth as it is in heaven.

In the spring of his thirty-third year, during the Jewish Passover celebration, Jesus was arrested by the religious authorities, put on trial in the middle of the night, and at their urging, sentenced to death by a Roman governor. On the day known to history as Good Friday, Jesus was crucified on a Roman cross. He was buried in a borrowed tomb. On the following Sunday, according to multiple eyewitness accounts, he was physically raised from the dead. He appeared to hundreds of people, taught his disciples, and prepared for what was to come.

Forty days after the resurrection, Jesus ascended bodily into the heavens where, according to the Bible, he sits at the right hand of God, as the Lord of heaven and earth. Ten days after his ascension, in a gathering of more than three thousand people on the Day of Pentecost, a Jewish day of celebration, something truly extraordinary happened. A loud and powerful wind swept over the people gathered. Pillars of what appeared to be fire descended upon the followers of Jesus. The Holy Spirit, the presence and power of God, filled the people, and the church was born. After this, the followers of Jesus went forth and began to do the very things Jesus did—preaching, teaching, and healing—planting churches and making disciples all over the world. Today, more than two thousand years later, the movement has reached us. This is the Great Awakening and it has never stopped.

Yes, two thousand years hence and more than two billion followers of Jesus later, this awakening movement of Jesus Christ and his church stands stronger than ever. Billions of ordinary people the world over have discovered in Jesus Christ an awakened life they never imagined possible. They have overcome challenges, defeated addictions, endured untenable hardships and suffering with unexplainable joy, and stared death in the face with the joyful confidence of eternal life. They have healed the sick, gathered the outcasts, embraced the oppressed, loved the poor, contended for justice, labored for peace, cared for the dying and, yes, even raised the dead.

We all face many challenges and problems. They are deeply personal, yet when joined together, they create enormous and complex chaos in the world, from our hearts to our homes to our churches and our cities. All of this chaos traces to two originating problems: sin and death. Sin, far beyond mere moral failure, describes the fundamental broken condition of every human being. Sin separates us from God and others, distorts and destroys our deepest identity as the image-bearers of God, and poses a fatal problem from which we cannot save ourselves. It results in an ever-diminishing quality of life and ultimately ends in eternal death. Because Jesus lived a life of sinless perfection, he is able to save us from sin and restore us to a right relationship with God, others, and ourselves. He did this through his sacrificial death on the cross on our behalf. Because Jesus rose from the dead, he is able to deliver us from death and bring us into a quality of life both eternal and unending.

This is the gospel of Jesus Christ: pardon from the penalty of sin, freedom from the power of sin, deliverance from the grip of death, and awakening to the supernatural empowerment of the Holy Spirit to live powerfully for the good of others and the glory of God. Jesus asks only that we acknowledge our broken selves as failed sinners, trust him as our Savior, and follow him as our Lord. Following Jesus does not mean an easy life; however, it does lead to a life of power and purpose, joy in the face of suffering, and profound, even world-changing, love for God and people.

All of this is admittedly a lot to take in. Remember, this is an invitation. Will you follow Jesus? Don't let the failings of his followers deter you. Come and see for yourself.

Here's a prayer to get you started:

> Our Father in heaven, it's me (say your name), I want to know you. I want to live an awakened life. I confess I am a sinner. I have failed myself, others, and you in many ways. I know you made me for a purpose and I want to fulfill that purpose with my one life. I want to follow Jesus

Christ. Jesus, thank you for the gift of your life and death and resurrection and ascension on my behalf. I want to walk in relationship with you as Savior and Lord. Would you lead me into the fullness and newness of life I was made for? I am ready to follow you. Come, Holy Spirit, and fill me with the love, power, and purposes of God. I pray these things by faith in the name of Jesus, amen.

It would be our privilege to help you get started and grow deeper in this awakened life of following Jesus. For some next steps and encouragements, visit seedbed.com/Awaken.

INTRODUCTION

Welcome to this daily reflection on the person and work of the Holy Spirit.

Many years ago, I had the privilege of meeting Gordon Fee, one of our generation's most important New Testament scholars. Fee's pastoral insights and explanations of the Holy Spirit are second to none. In his book, *Paul, the Spirit, and the People of God*, we find these penetrating words in the opening overture:

> The Spirit as an experienced and empowering reality was for Paul and his churches the key player in all of Christian life, from beginning to end. The Spirit covered the whole waterfront: power for life, growth, fruit, gifts, prayer, witness, and everything else. . . . If the church is going to be effective in our postmodern world, we need to stop paying mere lip service to the Spirit and to recapture Paul's perspective: the Spirit as the experienced, empowering return of God's own personal presence in and among us, who enables us to live as a radically eschatological people in the present world while we await the consummation. All the rest, including fruit and gifts (that is, ethical life and charismatic utterances in worship), serve to that end.[1]

For us to understand what it means to be a Christian is dependent upon our understanding of the dynamic, fresh work of the Holy Spirit. Without the Holy Spirit, there is truly no such thing as the Christian life. With the Holy Spirit, however, individuals

---

1. Gordon Fee, *Paul, the Spirit, and the People of God* (Grand Rapids: Baker Academic, 1996), xv.

and communities that follow Christ are empowered to become *like* Jesus in the world, incarnating both his way of being human and his method of expressing God's powerful love and personal presence in our world.

And there it is. If we neglect the Holy Spirit, we slowly, quietly lose our faith in a God who *acts* in and through us. But if we make it our intent to understand how the Holy Spirit is at work in us, through us, and in the world, then we are getting to the heart of what it means to be a follower of Jesus in our time. If you're holding this book in your hands, then I believe you've chosen the latter.

When I was first asked to write this daily devotional on receiving the Holy Spirit from Genesis to Revelation, my internal response was, *I think you have the wrong person.* Don't get me wrong, I delight in, I am enraptured by, and I am continually drawn to the Holy Spirit. I can't think of a more important topic to write about than what it means for a Christian to embrace the fullness of the Spirit's work in our lives, and then in the lives of others through Spirit-enabled acts of obedience.

But what I did find daunting was that the Holy Spirit is commonly spoken of, biblically, in the language of mystery and metaphor and I wasn't sure my words would do such a grand topic justice. Jesus himself says of the Spirit, in John 3:8, "The wind blows wherever it pleases. You hear its sound, but you cannot tell where it comes from or where it is going. So it is with everyone born of the Spirit." That is a beautiful way to describe how the Holy Spirit brings new life to the awakened heart—but the image itself puts us in the realm of the indescribable, the mysterious, and the unseen.

Then one day the Holy Spirit spoke to me; "Write about me in stories that reveal what I do. What I do speaks of who I am." I trust that what follows in this writing bears the tone of humility that I felt continually sounding in my heart as I wrote each reflection.

Let's look for what the Holy Spirit does in the Scriptures and in our lives, and in so doing, we can begin to discover more about who the Spirit is—and what it means to cooperate with the Spirit's ongoing work of transformation.

As we begin our journey together, please pray this prayer with me: Holy Spirit, I welcome you to open me to all you intend to speak to me and do in me through this season of reading. I receive you, Holy Spirit, as my companion and guide on this journey into the heart of God. I receive you and welcome you to guide me into fullness of life with Christ in the days and years ahead. Use me; I surrender to your loving guidance. I receive you, Holy Spirit. In Jesus' name, amen.

RECEIVE THE HOLY SPIRIT

JOHN 20:21–22

Again Jesus said, "Peace be with you! As the Father has
sent me, I am sending you." And with that he breathed
on them and said, "Receive the Holy Spirit."

Breathe in deeply with me for a moment. Now, breathe out. Feels
good, doesn't it? Our breath is unseen, but yet is so very, very real.
Breath and breathing are powerful, primal images for us as human
beings. To breathe is to be *alive*.

In the Bible, the Holy Spirit is understood to be God's very
breath—the pure expression of his sustaining, creating, and transforming life (Gen. 1:2). In the Nicene Creed, the Holy Spirit is
called "the giver of life." Anything we can and could say about
the Holy Spirit will always come back to the fact that the Spirit
is the breath, the wind—the living, active, creative, and life-giving
presence—of the Creator of the universe.

In John 20, the image of the Spirit as the breath of God comes
to the fore as Jesus steps into a room full of bewildered disciples
immediately following his resurrection. Can you imagine the
moment? Mary said she had seen the Lord (v. 18)—should they,
could they, believe her? As Jesus enters the room where they've
been hiding from the Jewish authorities (v. 19), they are suddenly

awakened from their unbelief, fear, and disillusionment—they are seeing Jesus alive before their very eyes!

He is *breathing* again, by the Spirit that raised him from the dead (Rom. 8:11). Their Lord was just recently *breath-less* on the cross; now he is standing in front of them *breath-full* and ready to provide divine resuscitation to any soul ready to rise with him! Jesus begins to speak, and in the same way Jesus spoke to the disciples in that room where their lives changed for good, so too our risen Lord walks into the room of our hearts, by the Spirit, and speaks these words to you and me today.

"Again Jesus said, 'Peace be with you!'" *Receive his comfort.*

"As the Father has sent me, I am sending you." *Receive his commission.*

"And with that he breathed on them and said, 'Receive the Holy Spirit.'" *Receive his life-giving blessing—his presence, strength, and hope for all your days ahead!*

So how about it? Are you ready to join the early disciples? Are you ready to receive the Holy Spirit? Are you ready to breathe more deeply the breath of God?

"Receive the Holy Spirit."

THE PRAYER

Jesus, I receive the Holy Spirit. Open me up to receive all you have for me. Come, Holy Spirit. I yield my heart to you as the disciples did, to receive the life-giving gift of your presence. I am ready for my own personal Pentecost. I receive your Holy Spirit. I pray in Jesus' name, amen.

DAN WILT

- Have you ever needed to catch a good, full breath? How did it feel when you felt that unseen air rush into your lungs?

- In what ways does that moment speak of what happened for the disciples in John 20—and what can happen in you if you open yourself now to receive the Holy Spirit?

LET'S COME TOGETHER FOR THE PARTY!

ACTS 2:1

When the day of Pentecost came, they were all together in one place.

Birthday parties are a big deal in our family; everyone makes a Herculean effort to be as together as we can be as each date rolls around on the calendar. Even when one of us is traveling on the other side of the world, we leverage modern technology to see each other, say a kind word or two, and (when I'm allowed by my resident nutritionist) eat cake.

When the Bible talks about miraculous events, there is often great care taken to tell us exactly who was there, *together*, when the event occurred. Why do the Scriptures seem to take attendance time and time again? When God acts powerfully on earth, *people* are the point—we are always either directly involved and/or directly impacted. Who is impacted, *together*, tells us something about why the event occurred.

And that brings us to Pentecost. For Christians, Pentecost is celebrated around the world as the moment in history that the body of Christ, the church, was Spirit-baptized and Spirit-born. In other words, we could say that Pentecost is the spiritual birthday of the

4

church. From the day the Holy Spirit filled those 120 believers in the Upper Room all those millennia ago, there has been a non-stop party commemorating the awakening that can only come when the Holy Spirit rushes into the human heart!

Who was *together*, in that upper party room, that amazing day of great awakening? From what we can glean from Acts 1:13–15, some 120 men, women, Mary (Jesus' mother), and Jesus' brothers were there. The sound of rushing wind, flames of fire, tongues in many languages, and a mass evangelism moment that set the Roman Empire reeling in its wake were all a part of the party. I would pay any ticket price for that multi-sensory immersion experience.

Think about it. They were no longer afraid of the Romans, *together*. They were no longer sad for their loss, *together*. They were yielded and energized and anticipating and expectant and alert and joyful and hopeful and fearless and praying and surrendered . . . *together*. They were ready to do "greater things than these" (John 14:12–14)—*together*. They were ready to show the hospitality of Christ to a waiting world, *together*. And now, they were being filled with and empowered by the Holy Spirit—*together*!

Are you ready, like the 120 who went before us on that first Pentecost, to receive the infilling of the Holy Spirit? Are you ready to receive the gift of that full-immersion experience for the sake of your own heart awakening, and for the awakening of hearts all around you? Are you ready, with the rest of us, to do what Jesus did—*together*?

THE PRAYER

Jesus, I receive the Holy Spirit. I am ready to take another step to receive spiritual gifts from you for the world around me. Come, Holy Spirit, fill my heart and the hearts of those in my community so, together, we can carry your message of unquenchable love to those within our reach. I pray in Jesus' name, amen.

THE QUESTIONS

- Have you ever experienced your own Pentecost moment where you believe you were filled with, and empowered by, the Holy Spirit?

- What was it like, and did it stir in you a desire for even more awareness of the Spirit's active presence in your life?

TORNADOES TEND TO MOVE THINGS AROUND

ACTS 2:2

Suddenly a sound like the blowing of a violent wind came from heaven and filled the whole house where they were sitting.

The sirens have gone off again. We grab our phones, continually beeping with weather alerts, and rush downstairs to our basement room. It's a small space with a solid door and a few food staples and water kept inside for just such an emergency as this.

A tornado is coming through our area, and for those who have experienced one of those untamed forces of nature, it's a terrifying thing. The sound alone tells you that an undeniable, irresistible, unseen force is right at your doorstep—and you'd better respect it because you simply cannot stop it!

When Luke is describing what happened on that first Pentecost Day in Acts 2, he chooses "a sound like the blowing of a violent wind" as his metaphor. The disciples heard a roar, probably like the sonic tumult made by a tornado, and the choice of the word "violent" or "strong" reveals the feeling he is seeking to convey—this is no light breeze we're dealing with here!

For the Jewish disciples, this kind of irresistible wind language related to the Spirit would have tied their stories together all the way back to the beginning of time. In Genesis 1, the Spirit (breath) of God hovers over the surface of the waters, bringing order to chaos, form to the formless. In Ezekiel 37:1–14, the prophet prophesies to the breath, the wind of God, and the valley of dry bones becomes a people filled with the Spirit of God. In John 3:8, Jesus refers to the wind when he talks about the Spirit coming and going, known only by the sound of its presence, like the wind.

Then, when Jesus breathes on his disciples in John 20:22 and tells them to "receive the Holy Spirit," Luke and every other disciple would have connected those words all the way back through salvation history to the very beginning of time.

Now, the wind of the Spirit that hovered over the surface of the abyss at creation is roaring in the Upper Room. God's powerful breath bringing order to chaos, life to a valley of dry bones, and strength to their fearful hearts is now filling them with power to be like Jesus in the world!

When the Spirit comes, hearts are filled with Jesus, who empowers us to be his ambassadors in our spheres of influence. And like a holy tornado, sometimes things are moved around that we wish were left in their place! But everything that the Holy Spirit does, the Holy Spirit does for our good—and the good of those around us.

THE PRAYER

Jesus, I receive the Holy Spirit. I am learning to welcome you to move in and through my life, no matter what gets moved around. Come, Holy Spirit. Have your way in my heart—I want to join you and your other followers in awakening the world to your love. I pray in Jesus' name, amen.

THE QUESTIONS

- What do you imagine the scene was in that Upper Room?

- Put yourself in the space with the disciples; what must it have felt like?

FILLED WITH THE FIRE OF LOVE

ACTS 2:3

They saw what seemed to be tongues of fire that separated and came to rest on each of them.

When people talk about the Holy Spirit in the language of being empowered by the presence of God actively moving within our hearts, many Christians across history have used the language of *fire* to describe the experience. Fire is also often used as a metaphor for love, and as we look at the Acts 2-motivated church in the New Testament, if there is one word that describes their lifestyle and sense of purpose, it is *love*.

If the Holy Spirit is God, and God is love as we are told in 1 John 4:7–13, we can begin to see the fire lighting on the disciples as the fire of heaven's unique kind of love filling them—for wholeness and for mission. A mission of *power* was not gripping their hearts. A mission of *love* was laying hold of them—a mission that first sought them, and then created a desire in them to seek others. The Spirit of Jesus was filling them—and his love was about to be the *source* of the miracles that would follow those who believed in his name.

Let's look at the Pentecost experience once again, seeing it through the lens of God's love.

The Upper Room is in a holy ruckus of the elements—a loud sound like a roaring wind is at level-10 volume, and now "tongues of fire" are floating in the air, seeming to separate and "come to rest" on each of them! What a sight! This is a full-on audio-visual worship experience the disciples are having together; they are being loved by God—body, mind, and soul—and that heavenly love is shaking the walls with its power.

The fire, like the sound of wind, is coming from "heaven" (v. 2), the place where Jesus is seated at the right hand of God. After ascending to the right hand of the Father just ten days earlier, fulfilling the words of Psalm 110:1, Jesus connects heaven and earth in a dynamic, new way. Heaven's winds are blowing, and heaven's fires are blazing as earth's people—the disciples—are being caught up in heaven's reality. A heaven-and-earth people are being born in a new way, those who are "seated in heavenly places" with Christ (Eph. 2:6) and who can now live and see things—heart and mind engaged—from a heavenly perspective (Col. 3:1–2).

Heaven and earth meet in a profound new way when the Spirit fills a person, and we begin to have the heart of God for ourselves and for others. If wind moves static things and gets still things in motion, fire addresses things that are cold and need warming, heating, energy. Love is the fire that burns in the heart of God for the world. The love of God is the greatest power in the cosmos—and when we are filled with the Holy Spirit, we are filled with the love of God for ourselves and others.

Jesus, I receive the Holy Spirit. You promised a full-immersion, heavenly baptism to your disciples, and I am invited to the same. Come, Holy Spirit, baptize me in your full, empowering presence. I am ready to be filled to overflowing with the fire of your love for the world around me. I pray in Jesus' name, amen.

THE QUESTIONS

- What teaching have you had about the baptism of the Holy Spirit?

- How does that impact how you see the Holy Spirit at work in your life right now?

- Do you want more of the Holy Spirit than you seem to be experiencing right now?

SPIRITUAL GIFTS ARE GIVEN FOR A REASON

ACTS 2:4–8, 11B

All of them were filled with the Holy Spirit and began to
speak in other tongues as the Spirit enabled them.

Now there were staying in Jerusalem God-fearing Jews from every nation
under heaven. When they heard this sound, a crowd came together in
bewilderment, because each one heard their own language being spoken.
Utterly amazed, they asked: "Aren't all these who are speaking Galileans?
Then how is it that each of us hears them in our native language?"...

"We hear them declaring the wonders of God in our own tongues!"

I like to say that I speak 1.25 languages—English and exactly one-fourth of the Spanish that I would need to speak to thrive in a Spanish-speaking country. After two years of Spanish in high school, and four years of study in university, I should be further along. But, deep down, I'd prefer to learn a second language like the disciples did in the Upper Room—via a sovereign gift from the Holy Spirit!

The disciples, experiencing the overwhelming and incomprehensible love of God for them in the Upper Room, tasting the glories of heaven while still on earth, begin to actually *do* something in response to the in-breaking of God's kingdom. Heaven and earth had open doors to one another, and the disciples began to speak in *tongues*. In other words, they began to speak in other existing languages they previously did not know.

Now, let's acknowledge that the spiritual gift of tongues is a hot topic in the wider body of Christ—who gets it, who doesn't, what it's for, what it's not for, if we should want it and ask for it, or if we should leave it in the "early church needed it" storage closet (until we can have a personal fireside chat with Jesus about it).

But there is an important point to be made here about this particular instance of speaking in tongues before we get lost in theological analysis. The Spirit of Jesus was filling them, yes, to transform them from the inside out and to give them spiritual power to live the Jesus-life. But the Holy Spirit was *also* filling them to give them power-from-beyond-themselves to be ambassadors, witnesses, of that very same love to the world God loves (John 3:16).

They were being empowered to be *Christophers*—Christ-bearers— to the very ends of the earth. In other words, as they received the fullness of the Holy Spirit that day, the Spirit gave them the gift of speaking in other tongues . . . wait for it . . . for *mission*.

Every gift has a giver and an intended recipient and, in this case, the end recipient of a spiritual gift was not the disciples; it was the mass of Jews from many nations coming together for the Pentecost festival. Pentecost was an historic harvest feast for the Jewish people (and still is)—and the ascended Jesus, by the Spirit and through his church—converts it into a festival for the harvest of souls to God!

With the Great Commission ringing in their hearts (Matthew 28:18–20a), the disciples begin to declare God's glory, God's wonders, in the languages of those gathered. And we know the end of the story—about three thousand were added to their numbers that day.

Here we discover a very important idea embedded in Holy Spirit history, and in how we are to understand spiritual gifts: *spiritual gifts exist to enable individual followers of Jesus to convey God's love to others in ways that awaken the heart, mind, and body to the love of God.*

THE PRAYER

Jesus, I receive the Holy Spirit. I am eager to be given spiritual gifts in moments when you want to do something profound in the life of another person. Come, Holy Spirit, turn my heart outward, toward the Great Commission you have given, that I would desire spiritual gifts to serve others coming to know you. I pray in Jesus' name, amen.

THE QUESTIONS

- Have you ever seen someone exercise a profound spiritual gift that became a pivot point for someone giving their heart to Jesus?

- What was it like, and what was the end result?

THE HOLY SPIRIT
IS AN ARTIST

GENESIS 1:1

In the beginning God created the heavens and the earth.

Before diving further into the Holy Spirit's work in the New Testament, it will be good for us to go back to the Old Testament, as the curtain opens on creation, where we are first introduced to the Spirit of God. Stepping deep into the past will help us see our present encounters with the Holy Spirit by the glow of a fresh, yet ancient light.

As the pen is ready in the writer's hand, and the book of Genesis is about to come to life, heaven's Author makes a *choice*. It is an artistic word-choice that God knows will frame for us his essential character—and will help us understand the ongoing nature of the Spirit's work.

"In the beginning God *created* . . ."

Let that verb, *created*, ring in your heart. The Spirit of God is *creative*. For God to be *creative* means that God is a *maker*—a masterful, astounding, and even playful artist of the most magnificent kind. And when the beauty that God the Artist creates, like you and I, becomes blemished, distorted, shamed, confused, or shattered, he moves into the mess (John 1:14) to guide the process of restoration until all things are made new (Rev. 21:5).

Many years ago I was at a worship event where individuals were invited to stand if they needed prayer. We were encouraged to not just pray for these women and men out of our human compassion, but to first be silent, together, to allow the Holy Spirit to speak to us before any talking or praying was done. I went over to a man that I felt prompted to pray for and asked if I could put my hand on his shoulder. He nodded yes and as I looked into his eyes I could see he was carrying some very heavy burdens.

We waited together, as brothers in Christ, in silence. After a few moments, I shared a scripture or two, and we waited a few more minutes. Then an image began to form in my mind, a moving picture of a black stallion, running across a beach. I sensed it was from the Lord, so I shared it with him. He immediately began to cry. I took that as a clue that the Holy Spirit was doing something in his heart that neither of us fully understood.

After praying together for twenty minutes, guided by this image and the scriptures and metaphors it evoked, we finished. The man opened his eyes and looked at me, his countenance now bright and a wide smile on his face. "Do you know what I do for a living?" he said. I shook my head no.

"I work with horses!" He went on. "Do you know what my favorite movie of all time is?" I had a wild guess. He said, "*The Black Stallion*"! We laughed out loud together at the creativity of the Holy Spirit—opening his heart to receive healing by showing a stranger his favorite movie! We were both humbled as we stood together, thanking God for his grace and goodness.

Creating and re-creating is God's way, the Spirit's *modus operandi*. We can expect the work of the Holy Spirit of God to always be both beautiful and *creative*—in us and through us.

THE QUESTION

- What is your favorite miracle in the Gospels and how do you see God's creativity at work as he draws hearts to himself?

THE BREATH THAT MAKES BEAUTY FROM CHAOS

GENESIS 1:2

Now the earth was formless and empty, darkness was over the surface
of the deep, and the Spirit of God was hovering over the waters.

In our home, we love the experience of listening to the wind blow
through the pine trees. We have a few pines in our backyard that
make a peaceful sound when the wind rushes through them. When
I am stressed or struggling, I will walk out the back door, listen for
that coniferous music, and talk to Jesus. If the wind is particularly strong that day, I will rush in the back door, voice raised,
declaring, "The wind in the pines is here! The wind in the pines is
here!" I'm no Paul Revere, but I can usually get at least one person
to come running.

There's a wind, a breath, that blows from the very center of the
universe into the seen and unseen world of creation. It is a wind
that moves galaxies on their paths, sustains life on the planet,
and whispers to us all from birth until death. It's not a physical
wind like the gentle breezes that stir the leaves of palm trees on
the islands of the Pacific, or a metaphorical wind like the "wind of
chance" that many people believe guides their destinies.

According to Genesis 1:2, that wind is the very *breath*, or in Hebrew, *ruakh*, of God. The *ruakh* of God is the word we translate *Spirit* (in Greek, the word is *pneuma* or *wind*). The *ruakh* of someone is the essence of their life, and God's Spirit, the Creator's living, active, dynamic presence, is in motion at the beginning of creation.

The Spirit of God is hovering over the waters of the great abyss—the desolation, the confusion, the emptiness. There is one word for those waters that captures all these themes in one package, and you and I are very familiar with it. That word is *chaos*. We've all known a little chaos in our lives, haven't we? Maybe today is no exception.

And this is when things get real. The Holy Spirit is an Artist, and when hovering over chaos, emptiness, and desolation, God's Spirit likes to move into the middle of the mess to *make beautiful* things, *meaningful* things, *ordered* things, out of the disorder.

The wind of the Spirit has been making a habit out of ordering chaos since the beginning of time—and is about that same business in your life and mine. When Jesus was awakened in the boat by the disciples, their emotions in turmoil because they feared a watery death, he spoke a word and calmed the chaotic sea. When Jesus confronted a gaggle of demons wreaking life-smothering havoc in a precious soul, he spoke a word into the chaos and brought the Father's loving order to a grateful heart.

A verse comes to mind: "Now the Lord is the Spirit, and where the Spirit of the Lord is, there is freedom" (2 Cor. 3:17). Lord, reveal to us what is "formless and empty" in our hearts so you can speak your word to it, your freeing, ordering word, awakening us to be the beautiful creations you intended us to be.

Jesus, I receive the Holy Spirit. There are some mighty messes in my heart and mind today that could use some cleanup. Come, Holy Spirit, breathe into each place of confusion and fear, and bring your loving order to my life. I pray in Jesus' name, amen.

THE QUESTION

- How is the Holy Spirit at work in your heart, home, church, or city—bringing beauty out of chaos?

YOU COME FROM GOD, AND GOD LOVES YOU

GENESIS 2:7

Then the LORD God formed a man [human being] from
the dust of the ground and breathed into his nostrils the
breath of life, and the man became a living being.

Moving through the Old Testament, we come upon one of the
most famous Holy Spirit verses in the Bible—Genesis 2:7. God is
breathing the breath of his Spirit, and it is bringing human beings
to life.

When my children were small, they were as inquisitive as one
would expect children to be. One night, while I was tucking one
of my daughters into bed, she abruptly asked me, "Daddy, where
do babies come from?" Her little eyes were beaming up at me, as if
her wise and all-knowing father would have the perfect answer to
her simple question.

I stumbled, wishing I had better prepared for this moment by
reading books like *How to Explain Complicated Things to Children
While Avoiding the Topic Altogether—Or at Least Pointing Them to
a Different Parent.* I blurted out my answer, based on Genesis 2:7:

"Well honey," I stuttered, "Babies come from God, and God loves his babies. You come from God, and God loves you!"

I know, you don't have to have a PhD in parenthood to come up with an answer like that. But my daughter showed her true Sunday school colors and believed me! She believed that what I said was *true* because she believed in *me*. She knew she was made and loved by God because she knew she was made and loved by me. A long explanation about biblical anthropology from Genesis 2:7 would have been accurate, but not effective. In this moment, *I* was the one loving her and that enabled her to believe that *God* loved her as well.

Sometimes we, as Christians, assume that people know they are glorious creations made in the image of God, and that the life-giving Spirit's breath is the singular reason their heart beats and their lungs process oxygen each day. But if we assume this, that people know the most basic truth that the loving Spirit gives them life, we are wrong. So many people in your sphere of influence and mine need to hear this simple, transforming truth: God's Spirit is giving them life, and he gives them life *because he loves them*.

The work of awakening is long, but is not as complicated as it may seem. "The thief comes only to steal and kill and destroy," Jesus said, "I have come that they may have life, and have it to the full" (John 10:10). Stealing souls from the enemy of our souls is the work of awakening, in prayer and action, and Jesus is leading the charge by his Holy Spirit in us.

Our hearts can become heavy when we realize, often in the place of prayer, that many people in our immediate neighborhoods are not aware they are loved by a God who cares about them more than they could ever comprehend.

If the church's one message was "You come from God, and God loves you!"—and we lived the kinds of lives that helped them believe that message could be true—we would see the signs of awakening for which we pray.

THE PRAYER

Jesus, I receive the Holy Spirit. To know that my heart is beating in this moment, and my lungs are filling as I read, is to know that I am not my own. I belong to you. Come, Holy Spirit, draw me into the work of showing those in my neighborhood that you love them, and that you have a purpose for their lives. I pray in Jesus' name, amen.

THE QUESTION

- Take a moment to feel your heartbeat. What does your heart beating tell you about God's love for you and his desire for you to carry his love to the world around you?

THE HOLY SPIRIT SUSTAINS ALL THINGS

GENESIS 2:1

Thus the heavens and the earth were completed in all their vast array.

The wonder and goodness of God's creation, especially as it is painted in Genesis 1 and 2, is truly astounding. And Revelation 4:11b affirms the sustaining source of this good creation: "For you created all things, and by your will they were created and have their being."

Day and night, waters above and waters below, land and seas, plants and trees, sun and moon, stars and star fields, fish and birds, beasts and rain and clouds and supernovas and snow flakes and beauty—including Spirit-born humankind—are all abounding, playing, rejoicing, in a world so bursting with majesty no one of us could ever take it all in.

And what keeps it all going? What keeps everything breathing, moving, orbiting, shining, growing, reproducing, providing, laughing, living, rising, blessing, and stirring admiration in our souls? The ancient Hebrew people understood that it is the Spirit of God who sustains it all (Ps. 104:27–30), keeping it in glorious, breathtaking *motion*.

Faith in Jesus Christ certainly concerns salvation when we die, and eternal life with God and one another in the new creation to come. It does indeed concern the powerful *redemptive* and *restorative* messages that find their center in Jesus and his gospel. But faith in Christ is also concerned with the powerful *meaning* and *purpose* messages that weave through a gospel that finds its roots in Genesis 1 and 2.

I have several people in my life who have taken to caring for various aspects of creation as their sense of life calling from God. My son says, whenever I recycle a can that I could just as easily have thrown into the trash, "Well done, Dad—you're doing the Lord's work!" Why does that ring true?

The Spirit's sustaining presence that keeps all of creation in motion, from the planets in our solar system orbiting the sun to the cow giving birth to a wobbly-legged calf, *values* what God has made. We've heard it said that God doesn't make junk. While I understand the sentiment of that phrase and how it could be helpful to someone with low esteem, I prefer to flip the idea around. God only and ever makes glorious, beloved reflections of his generous love!

"God saw all that he had made, and it was very good" (Gen. 1:31). Jesus sustains it by his word (Heb. 1:1–3). The Spirit *values* the creation! If the Trinity says it's good and it matters, so should we!

Join me in an exercise today. When you next walk out on your front porch, feeling the sun shining on your face and the light breeze brushing your face, thank the Holy Spirit for sustaining the world all around you! Thank the Holy Spirit for sustaining creation, and for giving you the privilege of walking in it, through it, and with it each day. Let your mealtime grace be filled with thanks for the provisions of the meal, the helping hands that touched each bit of it along the way to your table, and for the sustaining Spirit's goodness to provide for you in each season of your journey.

Thank you, Holy Spirit, for sustaining all things. Thank you, Holy Spirit, for sustaining me.

THE PRAYER

Jesus, I receive the Holy Spirit. You sustain all things around me, and keep this complex world alive at your loving command. Come, Holy Spirit, open me to truly see the glories of creation and your provision for me, that my thanks would spill over each new day you give me life. I pray in Jesus' name, amen.

THE QUESTIONS

- What aspects of creation most move you?

- Is there a particular experience you have had that made you aware that God is the sustaining presence behind all the world that is?

THE SPIRIT MEETS US IN OUR SLEEP

GENESIS 15:12A

As the sun was setting, Abram fell into a deep sleep, . . .

Early on in the Old Testament, we find the creative Spirit of God speaking to people in unique and often remarkable ways, ways that can help us understand how the Spirit can speak to us.

In Genesis 15:12, we find the Spirit of God speaking to the patriarch Abram in the nighttime hours. The story of Jesus, and the biblical imagination of the entire New Testament church, engaged the reality that the Holy Spirit speaks, at times, through dreams. God does this to further his new creation story and our growth as mature disciples and awakening people.

In the biblical narrative, sleep time is regarded as a normal part of life (Jesus was sleeping in a boat), yet also as a unique venue for the Holy Spirit to speak to individuals about the Father's heart for them and for the world (for example, Joseph's dream about taking Mary to be his wife). Sure, these people are the Son of God and a biblical hero, respectively. But does the Spirit speak to us normal Christians during the roughly thirty-three years we spend in bed over an eighty-ish year lifespan—or do we and the Trinity take those decades off?

In this story, Abram goes into a nap to end all naps (vv. 12–16) and something very profound happens. The Spirit of God speaks. The future is told. Promises are made. Then (we're not sure if Abram was asleep or awake for this part), a covenant is established through images familiar to Abram (15:17–21) that will connect all the way to the new covenant of Jesus and our faith in him today.

Across awakening history, dreams have been one way God gets his people's attention to pray at times and in ways we wouldn't have otherwise. Dreams can also serve as a way for God to give us experiences of his love and wisdom that we may not have otherwise. I know that I and many others have been stirred in the middle of the night with a strong urge to pray for a person or a situation, with an awareness of God's presence that is moving and restoring, or even with a song in the night that we find ourselves singing as we awake!

While we always need discernment in understanding dreams due to their subjective nature (supported by ongoing maturity in our walk with Jesus, reflection on the Scriptures, and the counsel of wise, discerning guides), it is true that the Spirit has something to say to us in the nighttime hours.

A wise woman of God once told me to keep a journal by my bed to write down dreams that felt important, either just for me or for others. The Spirit will begin to speak to you as you are going to sleep, through the night, and as you wake in the early morning hours . . . if you are expectant enough to keep a journal beside your bed. Read the Bible before you go to sleep to fill up your heart and mind with God's truth. Both you and God will know that you are eager to hear his Spirit speak if you keep that journal at the ready.

How about you? How has the Holy Spirit spoken to you in the night?

THE PRAYER

Jesus, I receive your Holy Spirit. I recognize that my sleeping hours, as well as my waking hours, are yours for the speaking. Come, Holy Spirit, speak to me in ways that remind me of your covenant love for me, and use my hours of rest to continue to transform me into the likeness of Jesus. I pray in Jesus' name, amen.

THE QUESTIONS

- Are you open to the Holy Spirit speaking to you, as the biblical characters were, in your nighttime hours?

- Grab a journal, and ask the Lord to speak to you as you go off to sleep.

THE SPIRIT HELPS US SAY "HERE I AM"

GENESIS 22:1–2

Some time later God tested Abraham. He said to him, "Abraham!"

"Here I am," he replied.

Then God said, "Take your son, your only son, whom you love—Isaac—and go to the region of Moriah. Sacrifice him there as a burnt offering on a mountain I will show you."

Pinnacle moments in salvation history, like this moment in Abraham's life, remind us that the Holy Spirit is at work helping us to say yes to the next act of obedience that will be required of us.

On any given day, our lives are progressing as normal. We are brushing our teeth, fixing our lunch, doing our work, paying our bills, navigating our relationships, making our decisions, answering our e-mails, and, then, BOOM. A test appears in front of us.

And that test is not like a math test in sixth grade, hard as that can be. The test we're talking about is a circumstance that occurs that requires a difficult, weighed decision from us. Often, that moment of decision can feel ultimate, defining, pivotal, and, according to what we choose, disrupting to our best-laid plans.

Abraham is going through life, tending his flocks, navigating marital challenges, experiencing the shock and joy of Isaac's birth, making treaties, swearing oaths, and, then, BOOM. A test appears in front of him.

He must make a decision as to whether or not he will obey the Lord's request for him to sacrifice his son. Isaac is not only his beloved boy; for the purposes of this test, Isaac is also the seed of God's promise to build a great nation through Abraham. This altar is one of supreme sacrifice, and Abraham has no way of knowing that there is a startling New Testament reason the Spirit is orchestrating this circumstance, recording this unique story of father-son sacrifice for all posterity, and welcoming Abraham to take a faith-leap that will be regarded by you and I as exemplary.

Did Abraham have any imagination for the idea that if he sacrificed his precious son, the only son shared between he and Sarah in their old age, that God would provide another child to them? Can we guess that Abraham, now sporting his new, "father of many nations" expanded moniker, would have been hosting a tremendous internal battle within, a deep and sleep-stealing spiritual confusion, as he quietly prepared to scale rocks and fields with his son that next morning? What did he say to Sarah at sunrise when she turned to him and asked, perhaps for the third time, "Where are you and Isaac going today?"

The Holy Spirit is at work in our lives, inviting us to acts of obedience that aren't heralded with the sound of trumpets and angelic fanfare. Obedience means that God asks something of us—to care for the person in front of us, share a word of encouragement with a difficult person, pray for a neighbor for healing, or to give a sacrificial gift of money to someone in need—and we make a quiet choice to say yes.

And we must do what Abraham did. We must show up. And if we're struggling, we must ask the Spirit to help us in our confusion and in our weakness (Rom. 8:24–26). Abraham's words of "Here I am" when God first speaks to him are converted from the "here I am" of "present and accounted for" to the "here I am" to do your will (Ps. 40:6–8; Heb. 10:9).

The Holy Spirit helps us say "Here I am" when God invites us to take a risk of faith.

THE PRAYER

Jesus, I receive your Holy Spirit. I know you may invite me to do something with you today that takes me out of my comfort zone. Come, Holy Spirit, and give me the strength and trust in that moment, to say "Here I am" to do your will. I pray in Jesus' name, amen.

THE QUESTIONS

- When is the last time you felt the Holy Spirit invited you to do something out of obedience, and you had little understanding of what the results might be?

- How did the situation turn out?

THE SPIRIT RUSHES TO A HUMBLE HEART

1 SAMUEL 16:13A

So Samuel took the horn of oil and anointed him in the presence of his brothers, and from that day on the Spirit of the LORD came powerfully upon David.

Discovering the work of the Holy Spirit throughout the Old Testament is a delightful process of scanning the Scriptures for the active presence of God. Like seeing vapor trails in the sky that show an airplane has passed that way, we can scan the sky of the Scriptures for signs of the Spirit's activity—moving back and forth through covenant history as we do.

In 1 Samuel 16, we meet David. David is first introduced to us as a shepherd, the youngest son of his father, Jesse (v. 12). We later discover that David is also a musician, singer, songwriter, and brave warrior (he is skilled with artillery, the proper category for the sling and the stones he used). He has been known to hang around sheep for extended periods of time, and to kill attacking lions and bears on an as-needed basis (1 Sam. 17:34–36). He'll take down the giant Goliath eventually, but that's not where our reflection is pointed today.

David's primary, Spirit-inviting character trait is seen at various points in his extremely up-and-down journey to wholeness and faithfulness. It's a trait that garners him the favor of the Lord throughout his lifetime. That trait is *humility*.

In 1 Samuel 16, the prophet Samuel shows up at Jesse's house after the Lord has rejected Saul as king. The Lord tells Samuel that it is one of Jesse's sons who will take his place. But when Samuel becomes impressed with a few of the young brothers standing before him, God famously says, "The LORD does not look at the things people look at. People look at the outward appearance, but the LORD looks at the heart" (v. 7b).

The Lord looks at the heart. Let's sit with that phrase for a moment.

David is called in from the field, and Samuel has found the Lord's anointed king. As Samuel is anointing young David with a horn of oil (oil symbolizing the Spirit in the Bible, and the presence of the Spirit on a person), the Spirit "came powerfully" on the new king as the anointed one. The Hebrew word for "came powerfully" actually can convey the meaning that the Spirit *rushed* on David (ESV), forcefully and unequivocally, empowering him for the life of obedience that was ahead.

The Lord looks at the heart. The Spirit rushes on David. Could these two ideas be connected? The Bible is not shy about revealing to us on whom the Spirit likes to reside. Yes, the Holy Spirit comes forcefully on David for the task ahead of him. But could it also be that the Spirit is rushing on David because the Spirit is actually *inclined* toward David? Is David, before he even starts his kingly journey, a "man after God's own heart" (Acts 13:22), with the kind of humility that recognizes who God is and who we are in his sight?

Humility is the character trait that opens David's heart to the Spirit, and the Spirit's heart to David. Humility will open up our relationship with the Spirit as well. The Spirit's presence rushes toward humility; the Lord gives grace to the humble (James 4:6; Prov. 3:34) and draws near to those whose heart is fully his (2 Chron. 16:9a).

Humility welcomes the Holy Spirit.

THE PRAYER

Jesus, I receive your Holy Spirit. I want to live in the humility of Christ, not considering equality with you something to be grasped, but becoming a servant of all (Phil. 2:1–11). Come, Holy Spirit, teach me the ways of humility so I become a resting place for your presence. I pray in Jesus' name, amen.

THE QUESTIONS

- How have you experienced God giving grace to the humble?

- Did you see that humility in someone else's life, or your own?

ALTARS OF WORSHIP AND THE MERCIES OF GOD

PSALM 51:10–12

Create in me a pure heart, O God, and renew a steadfast spirit within me.
Do not cast me from your presence or take your Holy Spirit from me. Restore
to me the joy of your salvation and grant me a willing spirit, to sustain me.

There are marked moments in our lifetimes, indelibly and internally etched in a Christian's memory, where we can each say with confidence: "God did this for me, and I was forever changed."

I like to imagine that each of us has a number of internal altars where, upon remembering a personal, transformative moment, we have the opportunity to kneel to give thanks again and again. Perhaps we built an internal altar when we experienced a moment of great success, a time when circumstances flowed in our favor and a deep sense of communion with God's Spirit was made all the sweeter by an advantageous result.

There are other moments, however, like those that preceded Psalm 51 in the life of David, where an internal altar was built because we experienced utter, divine *rescue*. And that rescue was not from an outward enemy—that rescue was from *ourselves*. We were headed in one direction, full and strong, and by the mercy of God, the Spirit brought revelation through our pain, our suffering, or as a sovereign gift of divine mercy. We were diverted from a path that led to death (Prov. 14:12), and we are so grateful that we were.

You may have some of those moments in your own life, and are visiting your internal altar of thanks even now. I know that I do. Feel free to pause here, and to sing a song of praise with me.

Psalm 51 is David's song of praise. It's a powerful, remarkable external expression of how grateful David was for the Holy Spirit, the Spirit who entered the chaos he had caused and saved him from himself. We know the story. David had sinned with Bathsheba. He had her husband Uriah murdered. He weaved a tangled web, and was using his power to justify it, fix it, and, ultimately, to hide it under a rug. He lacked accountability; he was the top of the food chain. Now, on the same track as all the royalty of his time, he was headed toward their fate, following unbridled lusts toward a hell of one's own making.

But one thing set David apart from all the others. David had the Holy Spirit at work in his life. David had a covenant with the God of Abraham, Isaac, and Jacob running through his mind and heart. David had the worship habits of his people ingraining truth into his dispositions and habits. David belonged to God— and the Spirit was making sure he didn't completely forget who he was and whose he was. The Spirit saw the chaos coming, and out of sheer mercy, stepped in to make something good out of it (Rom. 8:28). Nathan the prophet steps in, speaks by the Spirit, and David chooses to repent. Psalm 51 is the outer altar he builds for the inward altar of remembrance that is now set permanently in his soul.

Pray David's deep and enduring awakening prayer as your own today: "Do not . . . take your Holy Spirit from me." David was unwilling to go on without God's abiding presence searching his life, scanning his heart to expose wicked ways that lead to chaos and death, leading him into ways that are everlasting (Ps. 139:23–24). The Holy Spirit does this for us as well.

Do not take your Holy Spirit from me, O God. Your presence is life to me.

THE PRAYER

Jesus, I receive your Holy Spirit. I have so many altars in my heart coming to mind at which I can give you thanks! Thank you! Come, Holy Spirit, stir in me the steady songs of praise that will keep me singing, following you on the path that leads to life. I pray in Jesus' name, amen.

THE QUESTIONS

- Can you remember one of your altar moments when God rescued you from yourself?

- What words come to mind that you want to say to God in response to his Spirit's work on your behalf?

THE SPIRIT IS HERE, THERE, AND EVERYWHERE

PSALM 139:7-10

Where can I go from your Spirit? Where can I flee from your presence? If I go up to the heavens, you are there; if I make my bed in the depths, you are there. If I rise on the wings of the dawn, if I settle on the far side of the sea, even there your hand will guide me, your right hand will hold me fast.

There is a beautiful celestial object that glimmers in the night sky called the Orion Nebula. The Orion Nebula is the nearest "star factory" to Earth, and is a bright, stellar nursery where hundreds of new stars are being born. It is visible, in the best conditions, to the naked eye—unless there is light pollution, cloudy weather, or a problem with the eyes that are looking for it in the starry skies above.

The fascinating thing about the Orion Nebula is that no matter what the weather is like in my city, no matter at what point in the earth's rotation we are positioned, and no matter at what point in our revolution around the sun we are coasting, the object remains *there*. Anywhere you go in the world you can see it—if you wait long enough, look long enough, and know what to look for.

According to Psalm 139:7–10, that is how it is with the Holy Spirit. God's abiding presence is not determined by the weather in my heart that may obscure or reveal his loving activity in my life. God's pursuing presence is not determined by how I am feeling on this particular day of the year, or how I am faring during this particular season of my life. The Holy Spirit is always present, active, within reach, and *there*—if I have eyes to see.

Walking with the Holy Spirit through life can feel a bit like playing a very long game of hide and seek! One moment, we are sure of God's presence, our emotions in full connect and our minds at full attention. At other moments, however, we can feel very disconnected and unable to perceive God's presence. At those times, the Spirit is no less there, no less present, than ever before. But we can diminish in our awareness of the Holy Spirit's engagement with our lives if we are not practicing—cultivating through worship— an ongoing sense of his closeness.

Brother Lawrence, the seventeenth-century writer of the simple devotional classic, *The Practice of the Presence of God*, put it this way: "I make it my business to persevere in His holy presence, wherein I keep myself by a simple attention, and a general fond regard to God, which I may call an actual presence of God; or, to speak better, an habitual, silent, and secret conversation of the soul with God, which often causes me joys and raptures inwardly . . ."[2]

The Holy Spirit is not going anywhere—but we do. We can turn our hearts toward God at any moment, parting the clouds that obscure our awareness with a song of worship or a written prayer that stirs our soul, to enjoy a fresh conversation with the one who will never leave us or forsake us (Heb. 13:5b).

---

2. Brother Lawrence, *The Practice of the Presence of God* (Old Tappan: Spire Books, 1958), 36.

THE PRAYER

Jesus, I receive your Holy Spirit. You are present with me, right now, and your nearness is unchanging. Come, Holy Spirit, teach me how to cultivate an awareness of your love for me, and your intention to deepen me in faith and hope. I pray in Jesus' name, amen.

THE QUESTION

- Was there a time in this past month when God felt far away, but drawing near to God in worship seemed to close the gap?

LEAD ME, GOOD SPIRIT, TO BECOME LIKE JESUS

PSALM 143:10

Teach me to do your will, for you are my God; may
your good Spirit lead me on level ground.

It is a wonderful thing to know that because of the ascension of Christ we are "seated in the heavenly realms in Christ Jesus" (Eph. 2:6). Our reality is such that we are *here*, living out our days and nights on earth, and we are simultaneously *there*, living out our days and nights seated with Christ in heaven and learning what it is to be "like Jesus" in this world (1 John 4:17).

The Holy Spirit, according to Paul, is the Spirit of God's Son (Gal. 4:6; Phil. 1:19), and Jesus is at work in us daily—teaching us, instructing us, leading us—to become an awakened human being.

I have many family members and friends who are teachers. They instruct children, teenagers, and adults how to *do something*. The best of them teach those same children, teenagers, and adults not only how to *do something,* but how to *become someone* of character in the process.

The movement of the Christian life is into an ever-deepening learning process; we are learning at the core of our being to think

43

like Jesus, feel like Jesus, respond like Jesus, and become like Jesus in the world. There is no more essential definition of a Christian than this: someone who is becoming like Jesus. That is the highest compliment you or I could ever receive. That is what discipleship is all about. If discipleship becomes about anything else it will ultimately miss the mark and miss the point of why the Spirit indwells us in the first place.

At the same time we are learning, we are not starting this amazing transformation from scratch. We are filled with the Spirit of Jesus that we might have our heavenly classroom and our Teacher within—always available to us for a lesson or three!

When the psalmist wrote, "Teach me to do your will," and "May your good Spirit lead me on level ground," a powerful connection was being made with Jesus' words in John 16:13a, "But when he, the Spirit of truth, comes, he will guide you into all the truth."

Awakened people are those who have come to see Jesus not only as he is, but also as he is—and wants to be—in us. It is Christ's power at work in us that is energizing us (Col. 1:28–29) to become mature in Christ ourselves, and to turn and help others become mature in Christ as we go.

The Spirit is a good and benevolent teacher, coach, mentor, helping us make both decisions and disciples that lead to a church that evidences the love of Jesus to a love-hungry world.

THE PRAYER

Jesus, I receive your Holy Spirit. As a learner, with open hands and an open heart, I welcome you to instruct me in the ways of Christ. Come, Holy Spirit, train me to have the

DAN WILT

same compassion, wisdom, discernment, and confidence as my Lord. I pray in Jesus' name, amen.

THE QUESTIONS

- Who helped you understand how to become like Jesus in your own discipleship journey?

- In what ways are you helping others along that same path?

PRAISE IS FITTING WHEN THE SPIRIT IS MOVING

EXODUS 15:19–21

When Pharaoh's horses, chariots and horsemen went into the sea, the Lord brought the waters of the sea back over them, but the Israelites walked through the sea on dry ground. Then Miriam the prophet, Aaron's sister, took a timbrel in her hand, and all the women followed her, with timbrels and dancing. Miriam sang to them:

"Sing to the Lord, for he is highly exalted. Both horse and driver he has hurled into the sea."

The Old Testament makes a habit of directing glory to God, praised by his many names, when a major miracle has occurred. In those moments, we can understand the active presence of God, God's breath and wind, God's Spirit, moving circumstances to result in the deliverance, and in the delight, of human hearts.

In the case of Miriam, we see a woman caught up in ecstatic praise after the Egyptians are swallowed by the waters of the Red Sea. In Miriam's joy, leadership, and appropriate response to the Lord's great deliverance, we can see the Spirit of God at work in her inspiring a pure, unmitigated, emotion-rich, and vibrant act of *praise* within her community.

Praise. It's a worship word that is often used lightly in Christian settings as if we're actually doing the action it represents when we use the word, sing the word, or say the word in our prayers. But an act of praise remains quite different from a reference to praise. I can praise my wife for her kind character and gracious hospitality. I could also withhold praise by simply talking with her about what praise is, or by reciting praise of her that someone else has penned.

In the first case, I am deeply involved in what's happening—and she knows it. I am using words to help me engage in the act of praising her, and my intention adds weight to the meaning. In the second, I am participating in a form of praise, but withholding my own full engagement in the actual act of praise. In the former circumstance, I am a participant. In the latter, I am a spectator.

Miriam was engaged in an act of holy praise, spontaneously, and metaphorically combusting into a short season of delight, and thanks, and acclaim. And where the praise of God is igniting a spark from a pure heart, the Spirit is in the background, adding fuel and fanning it into flame. For those who withhold praise, managing appearance rather than offering appearance as a conjoined offering with praise, the Spirit is at work to open up those withholding hearts to joy.

When we see a work of God, it demands we stop and praise. A moment or a season of praise is appropriate and important when the Father is seen at work. The Spirit helps us praise—to engage your soul and mine in the wondrous worship of heaven.

THE PRAYER

Jesus, I receive your Holy Spirit. Let praise become my first language when I see the smallest acts of deliverance that come from your hand. Come, Holy Spirit, fan worship into flame within my heart, that praise may rise from these lips many times a day. I pray in Jesus' name, amen.

THE QUESTIONS

- What is your favorite song of praise, of acclaim, to God?

- Take a moment to sing it now, a few times, if possible, as an expression of appreciation for all that Jesus is doing in your life. Let the Spirit move you to praise as you sing.

WHEN A BURNING BUSH SPEAKS YOUR NAME

EXODUS 3:2–4

There the angel of the Lord appeared to him in flames of fire from within a bush. Moses saw that though the bush was on fire it did not burn up. So Moses thought, "I will go over and see this strange sight—why the bush does not burn up."

When the Lord saw that he had gone over to look, God called to him from within the bush, "Moses! Moses!"

And Moses said, "Here I am."

When the image of fire shows up in the Bible, it is often related to God's presence illuminating the way to freedom for his beloved people. God's presence has been associated with fire for a long time—fire in a bush (Ex. 3:2–4), fire in a pillar (13:21–22), fire on a mountain (19:18), and fire in a cloud (40:34–38).

By the time we get to Acts 2:1–4, we see the flame of God's presence is once again leading, lighting, and guiding the way to a new, empowered freedom of the heart. It's a personal burning bush moment for every disciple in that Upper Room.

Moses. Drawn out of the Nile River by the daughter of the great Pharaoh and raised as a treasured member of the ruling family, he was a Hebrew. Moses' daily regimen prepared him to become a great ruler, and when someone called his name, he knew they were calling a true prince of Egypt. "Moses was educated in all the wisdom of the Egyptians and was powerful in speech and action" (Acts 7:22). Moses is a born and bred leader—and he knows it.

One squabble, one murder, one speedy escape, one family, and a few decades later, we find Moses again—now tending his father-in-law's sheep in the wilderness on Mount Horeb. His previous life had probably lost its Egyptian luster and had, perhaps, fallen out of memory. But as a son of Egypt's royal household, he may have also carried within him a residual sense of call to greatness, to leadership, to *destiny*. Is it possible that in some way, shape, or form, Moses was still searching for his purpose in life? Is it possible that he was actively looking for someone to call his name as a son, to define his purpose, and to clarify his sense of identity?

His curiosity drew him to a remarkable burning bush, blazing just for him. God called his name from within the fire. Moses heard his name and responded—and the rest is holy history.

While we know Moses' experience on Mount Horeb is a unique and central event in salvation history, many people in my home, church, and city are waiting to experience their own burning bush moment of God's presence. They are longing to see God work, to hear God call their name—leading them to their identity and purpose as a human being. They are open, hungry, and searching for hope—whether they say they are or not. A power encounter with the God of heaven can open the doors to transformation like little else can.

And that's where we come in.

When we partner with the Holy Spirit, taking a faith risk to pray for a struggling neighbor, encouraging the store clerk with a word we believe God has given us for them, or giving generously (out of our lack) to someone in great need, we help to open a heart to the Holy Spirit. In partnership with the Spirit, we see a burning bush moment come into view for someone Jesus loves.

In that encounter with the Holy Spirit, and with you, God will often silently, powerfully, speak that person's name. He will say, in some way, "You are seen, you are known, and you are loved."

THE PRAYER

Jesus, I receive the Holy Spirit. Thank you for calling my name, and drawing me to your love. Come, Holy Spirit, use me to be a light to others who are needing to hear their name called by you into an awakened life. I pray in Jesus' name, amen.

THE QUESTIONS

- Is there someone coming to your mind right now that needs to have a burning bush encounter with Jesus?

- How can you pray for them right now, and participate with the Spirit in what God is already doing in their life?

THE RIGHT WORDS
AT THE RIGHT TIME

GENESIS 41:38

So Pharaoh asked them, "Can we find anyone like
this man, one in whom is the spirit of God?"

Joseph is an impressive character in the Bible. In his early years, he comes off as arrogant, receiving dreams from God where he is set up as lord over his brothers—dreams he felt compelled to share with them. That went well. He also had a stunning coat he wore that reminded everyone he was a favored son of his father. That colorful piece of fashion only seemed to add insult to injury for his scheming siblings. We know what happened next.

The plots, the pits, the problems, and the prisons that dotted the way to Joseph becoming the head vizier (like a prime minister) of Pharaoh's household were all used by God for a grand purpose. Joseph was being humbled, and was simultaneously learning how to *listen* to God.

All through his difficulties, something was happening in Joseph's heart that was making him more attuned to the Spirit's whispers. He was gaining an inner ability to distinguish God's voice, God's thoughts, from his own. He was also practicing hearing God's voice and sharing what he heard by interpreting dreams in prison before he ever got to Pharaoh.

When the moment of truth comes for Joseph in Genesis 41:1–40, he is brought before Pharaoh to interpret his dream. The Spirit leads him to a correct and startling interpretation, but he first prefaces that interpretation with a powerful statement of humility. "Joseph answered Pharaoh, 'It is not in me; God will give Pharaoh a favorable answer'" (v. 16).

This makes me think of the story of a woman who was visiting a favorite restaurant. She saw another woman she recognized as a regular, and sensed the Holy Spirit prompting her to go pray for her. So she took a deep breath, and bravely walked over, not knowing what she would say. The timing was just right—the other woman was so grateful and amazed that someone could have known she was in need. They prayed together right then and there about some very challenging situations, and God answered the specific prayers they prayed in a profound way. A divinely orchestrated friendship began because someone discerned the Spirit's voice speaking within.[3]

Today, you and I as followers of Jesus, filled with the Holy Spirit, will have many opportunities to hear the Father speaking to us about someone near us—and something he wants to do in that person's life. If we will stay close to Jesus and nurture a listening relationship with him through worship, his Word, and through

3. This story can be read in its entirety in Vineyard Resources. *Come Holy Spirit: Stories of Ordinary People Partnering with an Extraordinary God* (Stafford: Vineyard Resources, 2019), 28–29.

moments of taking risks acting on what we hear, we, too, will be used by God to say the right words at the right time.

THE PRAYER

Jesus, I receive the Holy Spirit. If there are ways you want to use me as one of your listening disciples, ready to convey your love, then here I am—use me. Come, Holy Spirit, give me faith to step out, to take a risk today to partner with you in something special and miraculous. I pray in Jesus' name, amen.

THE QUESTIONS

- Could you imagine yourself listening more frequently, more attentively, in your heart, for something the Holy Spirit may want to give you for someone else?

- Are you willing to take a faith risk with Jesus today?

THE SPIRIT IS AT WORK THROUGH YOUR SKILLS

EXODUS 31:1–6

Then the LORD said to Moses, "See, I have chosen Bezalel son of Uri, the son of Hur, of the tribe of Judah, and I have filled him with the Spirit of God, with wisdom, with understanding, with knowledge and with all kinds of skills—to make artistic designs for work in gold, silver and bronze, to cut and set stones, to work in wood, and to engage in all kinds of crafts. Moreover, I have appointed Oholiab son of Ahisamak, of the tribe of Dan, to help him. Also I have given ability to all the skilled workers to make everything I have commanded you . . ."

We're moving around the Old Testament, scanning back and forth, searching for Holy Spirit truth. Like explorers, we're parting the dense brush of familiar biblical stories, looking deeper into each one for fresh insight into the nature and work of the Holy Spirit. With every discovery, we are adding to our broadening vision of how the Spirit works through you and me today, as awakened people, to accomplish the gospel goals that stir in the Father's heart.

According to Exodus 31:1–6, the opening story of Bezalel and Oholiab, the Holy Spirit accomplishes the will of God by working through, and with, our *skills*. Hmm. Our skills? Do you mean the Spirit uses the skills we loved learning, hated learning, learned because we had to, paid good money to learn, learned over decades, learned over a few weeks, or learned through the school of hard knocks?

The Spirit works through our *work*. The Spirit works through our *experience*. The Spirit works through our studied, rhythmic, informed, planned, deliberate, and habit-formed *actions*. We learn from this passage that not all gifts from the Holy Spirit fall easily into the categories of "spontaneous," "surprising," or even "miraculous" (as some would conceive). Sometimes the Spirit's presence is manifested through a person's inspired application of wisdom and learning, accrued over decades, and given heavenly impetus for the accomplishment of a particular task.

Perhaps you are a parent, educator, artist, teacher, health care worker, pastor, politician, or coach who is bringing your years of study, experience, and skill to a task given you by God. The Spirit fills those who follow God's loving invitation into the long, hard, and disciplined work of *preparation* for service. He strengthens our character through challenging seasons of training, and then uses the package of our heart and skills to accomplish his will.

First, we are told that Bezalel is "chosen" (v. 2). Second, we learn that Bezalel is "filled . . . with the Spirit of God" (v. 3), expressed in wisdom, understanding, knowledge, and skills. Third, we learn that Bezalel and Oholiab are given the "ability to teach others" (35:34), turning their skills not only toward their task—but also toward the mentoring and discipleship of others.

Strengthen the skills given to you by God, as an ongoing act of worship. Yield your talents and their development to the Holy Spirit along your journey. Then, keep a listening ear to heaven for the *kairos* moments the Father speaks, "Here. Now. I have filled you with my Spirit for this task." Do what God has given you to do—then devote yourself to training others to do the same.

THE PRAYER

Jesus, I receive your Holy Spirit. I yield the years of my learning, growing, and experiencing life to you. Come, Holy Spirit, help me to perceive your presence at work as I serve others with my skills, and help me to train and encourage others to do the same. I pray in Jesus' name, amen.

THE QUESTIONS

- What skills has the Lord been inviting you to hone over your lifetime so far, and in what ways has he invited you to use those skills?

- Can you think of other disciples in history whose training prepared them for a moment when God used them powerfully?

THE SPIRIT ORCHESTRATES YOUR SUCH-A-TIME-AS-THIS MOMENTS

ESTHER 4:12–14

When Esther's words were reported to Mordecai, he sent back this answer: "Do not think that because you are in the king's house you alone of all the Jews will escape. For if you remain silent at this time, relief and deliverance for the Jews will arise from another place, but you and your father's family will perish. And who knows but that you have come to your royal position for such a time as this?"

I love to listen to orchestras, especially when they are playing a movie soundtrack that moves me to tears. An orchestrator is the master *behind* the orchestra's music, a skilled musician who has the capacity to organize instruments, timing, and notes to make the elements of a piece of music *align*—and come to life. The orchestrator knows how the music should start, where tensions should build, where to offer releases that provide relief, and, finally, where the music should leave us at the end of our journey.

In other words, the orchestrator is the mastermind behind the whole experience—the one who makes sure that I cry by the end of the piece.

In our lives, heaven's Great Orchestrator, the Holy Spirit, coordinates timing (using millennia, centuries, decades, years, days, minutes, and moments) and instruments (ordinary people like you and me) to create masterpieces. The Spirit's creative compositions in your life and mine accomplish the Father's will. You and I are collecting amazing stories of God's faithfulness that we have often only appreciated for their beauty at the end of each story—after all the seemingly disparate pieces have come together.

In the moving biblical story of Esther, a young Jewish woman finds herself at the center of a great deliverance of her people. We sense God tending to the masterwork behind the scenes, orchestrating, coordinating, and administrating the rescue of his people. The instruments in this particular orchestration are Esther (our hero), her cousin Mordecai (her encourager), King Ahasuerus (the power broker), and his vizier, Haman (the ill-fated plotter and all-around bad guy). Each person was participating in a story through which God would reveal his love to a thousand generations (Deut. 7:9)—using the confusing affairs, plots, and actions of sin-struck humankind to create his masterpiece.

Interestingly, the activity of the Spirit of God is assumed in the book of Esther without explicit mention, which is often the way the Spirit seems to work in your life and mine—virtually incognito and in the most subtle of ways!

What do we discover about the Holy Spirit in Esther's story? We discover that the Spirit has expert timing; your God is moving in your present in ways that will one day make your past and future make sense. We have decisions to make, acts of courage to accomplish. But along the way, the Holy Spirit is working through it all.

Today, as people seeking to live a life awakened to Jesus, you and I will either have a such-a-time-as-this moment, or be on our way to one! Can you see the Holy Spirit active behind the scenes of today's challenges, using you as an instrument that will result in his glory?

Jesus, I receive the Holy Spirit. You are orchestrating my life in ways that I could never imagine. Come, Holy Spirit, I know that you are bringing together all things for my good—and the good of others around me. I pray in Jesus' name, amen.

THE QUESTIONS

- Have you ever experienced a confusing situation in which you only later saw the Spirit's orchestration of people, timing, and events?

- Knowing that, how should you respond to the current situations in your life that seem to be out of God's control?

THE SPIRIT, POWER, AND LEADERSHIP

JUDGES 4:14

Then Deborah said to Barak, "Go! This is the day the LORD has given Sisera into your hands. Has not the LORD gone ahead of you?" So Barak went down Mount Tabor, with ten thousand men following him.

The entire book of Judges in the Old Testament records great exploits and deeds done in the service of Israel's God and Israel's people. In Judges, when the Spirit of God is mentioned, themes we often associate with power—strength, courage, and decisiveness—are usually running through the text nearby.

With our modern sensibilities, we sometimes prefer to emphasize the Spirit-rich themes of love and compassion. But the Spirit of God is always at work in the spiritually awakened leader, shaping the power we have been given to become more like the power the Father expresses (and Jesus modeled). It is a love-rooted authority expressed in discerning, decisive action.

Let's get the picture. After Moses, Joshua is in the lead. He is filled with the "spirit of wisdom" (Deut. 34:9) by the laying on of Moses' hands (let's make a mental note of this physical sign of a transfer of blessing). Then, Joshua passes on, as does his whole generation of leaders—leaving the Israelites to run spiritually *wild*.

They are forsaking the God of Israel, and the Lord allows raiding parties from other nations to attack the Israelites.

Following soon after Joshua, and before the more famous Gideon and Samson come on the scene, the judge Deborah appears in Judges 4. Deborah exerts prophetic *leadership* (she is a prophet; v. 4). She is schooled in hearing the Spirit, and as she sits under a palm tree, she is learning to discern the best approaches to settling disputes among arguing Israelites (v. 5).

In other words, Deborah has practiced following the leading of the Spirit in small things—and will exercise that honed discernment in a bigger arena. Deborah is a listening leader, and that is where her spiritual authority comes from. Leaders who lead by learning the art of spending deep time listening to the Holy Spirit will not only lead by God's initiative, they will also intuitively know the frailness of leading from their own pastoral, corporate, or best practices experience. They rely on hearing God, and they trust the decisions that come from Holy Spirit discernment.

Deborah hears God speak and issues the words she receives. Then, in the name of the God of Israel, she exerts decisive, commanding, and, as we see in Judges 4:14–15, appropriately authoritative leadership. "Go!" is the command she hears from God. "This day . . ." is the timing she senses is appropriate. "Has not the Lord gone ahead of you?" is the promise reclaimed and remembered.

Leadership is a gift of the Holy Spirit, expressed in a variety of forms throughout covenant history. That leadership gift can be prophetic, pastoral, administrative, creative, apostolic, wise, and insightful—or expressed in other ways. If that leadership is motivated by love and continually surrendered to our Maker, the power one wields will heal rather than harm, liberate rather than oppress. Jesus had all the power in the cosmos at his disposal, yet the love that was its foundation directed its energies toward the freeing of the heart and the transformation of the soul.

To be a leader means to have influence. What we do with that influence is the question. Kingdom leadership is designed to thrive when submitted to the loving motivations of God and surrendered in discernment to the Holy Spirit.

Practice listening to the Holy Spirit in the little things, whether you lead in your home, your church, or your city—and you'll hear the Holy Spirit guide you when the stakes are high.

THE PRAYER

Jesus, I receive the Holy Spirit. I am eager to be a leader after your heart, leading from love and listening to your guidance. Come, Holy Spirit, fill me with wisdom, understanding, and courage for the moments of influence ahead. I pray in Jesus' name, amen.

THE QUESTIONS

- Have you ever had to act in confidence in a moment of leadership and found that the Holy Spirit was backing your initiative?

- What motive was in your heart as you took your step of courage?

HOMECOMING IS THE SPIRIT'S GOAL

EZEKIEL 36:26–27

"I will give you a new heart and put a new spirit in you; I will remove from you your heart of stone and give you a heart of flesh. And I will put my Spirit in you and move you to follow my decrees and be careful to keep my laws."

The prophets of the Old Testament were well-acquainted with the activity of the Holy Spirit. Prophets had the task of hearing the Spirit speak, and then delivering that undiluted message to the appropriate party.

The Hebrew word for prophesy is *naba*, and it means to speak (or even sing) by inspiration, or as I like to call it, "in-Spirit-ation." And what does the Spirit say? The Spirit is always drawing us back to our covenant-relationship with God. For a prophet like Ezekiel, the Spirit was inspiring him to call Israel *home*. A new heart, tender to God, is the homecoming gift for the exile in return, a heart of flesh that is responsive to the tireless love of God. The Spirit is always, always, calling people *home*.

Many years ago, I was sitting on an airplane getting ready to take off across the country. I was a happy introvert. It was a five-hour trip and the seat beside me—possibly the last open seat on the plane—was empty! Then, just as the doors were about to close and my restful journey was about to begin, a loud, angry, and large business man came bustling through the aircraft door.

He strode toward the back of the plane, right where I had settled in, and climbed over me to take the seat beside me (banging my head with his briefcase on the way through!).

Within moments, he was asking me if I believed in God! I had no Bible in my hand or "pastor" label stamped on my forehead. Then he launched right into his story: he told me how he had taken lives in the military, how he had tried to cleanse his guilt by doing humanitarian work, how he was an atheist, and how he hated God because his young daughter was dying in a hospital bed. (Note: his little girl regularly went and prayed for all the other patients on her floor. A sweet messenger had been given to him to help guide him home!)

In the middle of his confession, which had drawn the interest of everyone in the last five rows of the plane, I asked the Holy Spirit to speak to me. An unusual idea came into my mind: *Ask him who Rebecca is, and what her place is in his life.* I was terrified I would sound like a crazy person, but I went for it anyway. I told him that I believed God speaks to people, and whispered the question to him: "Who is Rebecca, and what place does she have in your life?"

His jaw immediately dropped. His eyes welled up with tears. His countenance softened. His voice fell to a whisper. "How do you know Rebecca?" he asked with unbelief.

"I don't," I said, "but God does, and he knows you too." Rebecca was his girlfriend, and she was trying to get them to go back to church. As we got off the flight, he promised me he was going to give God another chance.

As J. D. Walt says, the prayer we are invited to pray is "Jesus, I belong to you." And to own that prayer, sometimes a heart must be softened by an encounter that enables one to say: "Jesus, I am known and seen by you." To partner with the Holy Spirit, is to call people *home*.

THE PRAYER

Jesus, I receive the Holy Spirit. I want to partner with your Holy Spirit in calling people home to your great love for them. Come, Holy Spirit, teach me to hear your voice, and to obey. I pray in Jesus' name, amen.

THE QUESTIONS

- What are the names of those in your sphere of influence who come to mind as candidates for being called home to Jesus?

- Ask Jesus right now to do whatever it takes to turn them around.

A PEOPLE WHERE HEAVEN AND EARTH MEET

EXODUS 19:4–6A

"You yourselves have seen what I did to Egypt, and how I carried
you on eagles' wings and brought you to myself. Now if you obey
me fully and keep my covenant, then out of all nations you will
be my treasured possession. Although the whole earth is mine,
you will be for me a kingdom of priests and a holy nation."

As we slowly begin to turn toward the New Testament in our explo-
ration of what it means to "receive the Holy Spirit" (John 20:22),
there is a major Old Testament idea that we must consider. It sets
the stage for what it means for followers of Jesus to be Spirit-
empowered people in every generation. This big idea—the idea of
the *royal priesthood*—means that we are a people in whom *heaven
and earth meet.* To be filled with the Holy Spirit means that we have
a special priestly role to fulfill as Jesus' disciples in the world.

In Exodus 19, a beautiful calling is placed on the people of Israel,
from the oldest to the youngest. The Creator has chosen them
from among all of humanity, saying, "you will be my treasured
possession." Because of their sheer belovedness and God's great
affection toward them, they will be carried on "eagles' wings" to
be drawn into increasing intimacy with the great I Am. This people

and their God will share a mutual bond marked by *hesed* (covenant lovingkindness)—for all time.

The entire nation, God intended, would be a set-apart people who would communicate to the nations of the world that God is with us, for us, and on our side. In other words, they would be an entire kingdom of *priests*—every last one of them. While this may be a challenging idea for our modern mind to comprehend, it is worth a few moments to reflect on what God's intention for the royal priesthood would be, from Adam and Eve to you and me.

In the biblical ideal, a "priest" is a holy, set-apart one, a true meeting place of heaven and earth, an image-bearing, human sanctuary who embodies unbroken worship and unceasing covenant loyalty. A priest is to be one who, anointed by the Spirit, nurtures and facilitates the connection between God and people. A priest is to take another's hand to guide the way to wholeness in relationship with God. A priest is to lead a heart to embrace God's great story of rescue and restoration—with all its personal and corporate implications. A priest is one who calls God's people to worship in spirit and in truth, to maintain covenant love, and to thereby resist idolatry—and the injustice, dehumanization, and spiritual disorientation that inevitably follows it.

A priest is a worshiper of the true and living God, and leads others to become the same. A priest, in the New Testament, is a temple of the Holy Spirit (1 Cor. 6:10), and Jesus is our great High Priest (Heb. 4:14–16).

First Peter 2:9 speaks directly to us at this point, saying: "But you are a chosen people, a royal priesthood, a holy nation, God's special possession, that you may declare the praises of him who called you out of darkness into his wonderful light."

With the coming of the Holy Spirit to empower us, and with Jesus our Great High Priest dwelling within us, today we as "royal priests" are to guide others to maturity in Christ as they take their place in the royal priesthood alongside us. The Spirit of God is ever-watchful over our calling to be a royal priesthood, moving us toward maturity as heaven-meets-earth people.

Every spiritual gift, every Spirit empowerment given to the church, is designed to help us become those royal priests—bringing others back into covenant with their heavenly Father.

THE PRAYER

Jesus, I receive the Holy Spirit. I welcome the calling to become your royal priest, bridging the gap between others and your love. Come, Holy Spirit, fill me today with love and power to lead others into the divine healing and intimacy you have intended for them. I pray in Jesus' name, amen.

THE QUESTIONS

- Have you ever seen yourself as a place where heaven and earth meet?

- If not, what could you begin to do to nurture that understanding in your heart?

THE OUTPOURED SPIRIT OF GOD

JOEL 2:28–29, 32A

"And afterward, I will pour out my Spirit on all people. Your sons
and daughters will prophesy, your old men will dream dreams,
your young men will see visions. Even on my servants, both men
and women, I will pour out my Spirit in those days. . . .

And everyone who calls on the name of the LORD will be saved."

If I say the phrase, "I believe in God the Father Almighty, Creator
of Heaven and Earth," you may be tempted to mentally finish
with, "and in Jesus Christ, his only Son, our Lord." If you know the
Apostles' Creed, just a few words will trigger your memory of the
entire statement of faith.

Peter understood this same principle in Acts 2 when he chose to
launch his Pentecost day message with a well-known passage from
the prophet Joel. Michelangelo painted the prophet Joel on the
Sistine Chapel ceiling and I'm so glad he did. If any minor prophet
deserved it, it's Joel. Joel will forever be known to history as the
"Prophet of the Outpoured Spirit."

With perhaps thousands standing before him, Peter, a simple fish-
erman schooled in the way of Jesus by the Master himself, selects
Joel's words as his opening quote. He knows what this passage will

ignite in the hearts and minds of his people, bringing an entire section and theme of the Scriptures to mind. For Peter, Joel's message is a fire in his bones.

After a priceless moment of comedic timing (humor can be quite disarming, and I think that is what is happening with Acts 2:15), Peter begins. "In the last days," he quotes, "I will pour out my Spirit on all people."

Joel 2? His listeners probably thought, *I know this one!* Their minds must have begun to race as he recited the rest of the passage—a passage about the coming Day of the Lord.

Each devout Jew may have mentally scrolled back to the enduring homecoming commands of Joel 2:12–13: "'Even now,' declares the LORD, 'return to me with all your heart, with fasting and weeping and mourning. Rend your heart and not your garments. Return to the LORD your God, for he is gracious and compassionate, slow to anger and abounding in love . . .'"

"Return to me . . . Rend your heart . . . Return to the LORD your God" (i.e., turn around). Come home from your long exile. Empty yourself of your sin and what you've known. Come to the Lord with your freshly opened heart and "I will pour out my Spirit" on your sons, your daughters, all men and women. *"I will pour out my Spirit."*

Can you imagine the scene that followed next? Disciples scurrying everywhere, with about three thousand choosing to be baptized and to receive the Holy Spirit! The fields, Jesus said, are "white for harvest" (John 4:35 ESV)—and the beautiful new harvest festival we now call Pentecost was proof.

Joel finishes with: "The promise is for you and your children and for all who are far off—for all whom the Lord our God will call" (Acts 2:39). Joel's promise was not only for them, but for all who the Lord would call (Rom. 10:13)—you and I, the adopted sons and daughters of God (Eph. 1:3–6).

THE PRAYER

Jesus, I receive the Holy Spirit. I come to this moment with my heart open, returning to you in a new way, prepared to repent of all that stands in the way of me knowing you as I am known by you. Come, Holy Spirit, I am ready to be a Spirit-filled disciple. Jesus, I belong to you. I pray in Jesus' name, amen.

THE QUESTIONS

- Where in your journey with the Holy Spirit are you?

- Is there anything in the way of your relationship with Jesus that is ready to be set aside/offered to God so you can receive the fullness of his Holy Spirit working in and through you?

THE SPIRIT OF THE LORD WILL REST ON HIM

ISAIAH 11:1–3

A shoot will come up from the stump of Jesse; from his roots a Branch
will bear fruit. The Spirit of the LORD will rest on him—the Spirit of wisdom
and of understanding, the Spirit of counsel and of might, the Spirit of the
knowledge and fear of the LORD—and he will delight in the fear of the LORD.

In ancient times, an artistic process called "illumination" was
applied to special, often sacred texts. I'll admit, I'm a big fan of
the art form. The words of a document, placed largely in the
center of the page, are then surrounded by small paintings,
colorful calligraphic borders, and fine, decorative details in the
margins framing the piece (sometimes using real gold and silver).
Illumination would visually expand the written work on the page,
raising its sense of value and beauty in the process.

The magnificent words of Isaiah the prophet have illuminated
the Gospels (metaphorically, of course) for millennia. We could
almost put Isaiah 11:1–3 in the margins around everything Jesus
did and said in the Gospels. The uncanny accuracy, the sheer
power of each statement the book of Isaiah makes about the
coming Messiah, paints a picture of Jesus that clarifies his role in
ways that enhance and enlarge the living stories of Matthew, Mark,
Luke, and John.

"A shoot will come up from the stump of Jesse," rising from the roots, and this "Branch will bear fruit." "The Spirit of the LORD will rest on him"—his life an open, abiding place for the Spirit of God to find a fitting home. And, then, all sorts of beautiful things will begin to happen.

Wisdom will shine through his words. *Understanding* of himself, others, and the seen and unseen world around him will color his actions and speech. *Counsel* will flow from the Father through the clear conduit of his heart, making his bondage-breaking touch one that brings profound deliverance. *Might* will be expressed in love, and though he could exert strength by calling on legions of angels, he enlists the strength-guiding powers of compassion, mercy, and restraint. *Knowledge* will be at his fingertips. *Reverence and awe,* the fear of the Lord, will be the tones sounding within every message he gives.

And tying this all together? *Delight.* Jesus will delight in offering everything—all the wisdom, all the understanding, all the counsel, all the might, all the knowledge, and all the reverence—to bring glory to his Father (John 17:4).

Where does this same Spirit reside? For the follower of Jesus, in you and in me (2 Tim. 1:14). Called to be like him in this world (1 John 4:17), the Spirit empowers us to express Jesus' ministry with transcendent love, partnering with the Father in the dismantling of the works of the evil one (1 John 3:8).

Followers of Jesus are filled with the Holy Spirit so we can live and delight in a Jesus-kind of wisdom, understanding, counsel, strength, knowledge, and reverence. He is our North Star for daily living. "And we all, who with unveiled faces contemplate the Lord's glory, are being transformed into his image with ever-increasing glory, which comes from the Lord, who is the Spirit" (2 Cor. 3:18). Jesus is our North Star for daily living.

THE PRAYER

Jesus, I receive the Holy Spirit. I want to live faithfully, moved by the wisdom, understanding, counsel, strength, knowledge, and reverence that comes from you. Come, Holy Spirit, I yield myself to be transformed into the likeness of Christ. I pray in Jesus' name, amen.

THE QUESTION

- Choose one word or phrase mentioned in today's entry that connects with your life right now. In what ways have you seen yourself thriving in this area of your discipleship?

THE SPIRIT BEHIND THE GOOD NEWS

ISAIAH 61:1–2A

The Spirit of the Sovereign LORD is on me, because the LORD has anointed me to proclaim good news to the poor. He has sent me to bind up the brokenhearted, to proclaim freedom for the captives and release from darkness for the prisoners, to proclaim the year of the LORD's favor.

Isaiah 61:1–2a opens our eyes to a breathtaking vista of the person and work of the Holy Spirit. Isaiah the prophet comes through again, with the word of the Lord. This Old Testament passage lies at the center of a pivotal moment in Jesus' ministry in the Gospel of Luke, and reveals just how the Spirit behind the good news works.

Our Lord is invited to read from Isaiah in his local synagogue in Nazareth where he grew up (Luke 4:16–21). The room is probably packed. News about his teaching and miracles has been spreading. It's possible that the room is filled with the faithful, the curious, and the cynical. "Maybe a miracle or two would determine which of us is right about Jesus? I've heard he performs them in other places; I'd like to see one myself!"

Jesus, a hometown boy in a hometown synagogue, is handed the scroll. He opens it, and Isaiah 61 is his passage of choice. It is a prophecy about the Holy Spirit resting on God's Messiah. He knows the stir it will cause if he reads it. But he has just come out of the desert having fasted and faced down the Accuser of all of our souls. He is filled with the power of the Spirit after that encounter (Luke 4:14)—he is filled with resolve . . . with focus. Jesus didn't come this far to turn back now simply because he is being quietly scrutinized by his entire hometown.

"The Spirit of the Sovereign LORD is on me . . ." He finishes the passage. Can you feel the drama? You could have heard a pin drop. He sits down. The room is silent, and staring. Then, he says it: "Today this scripture is fulfilled in your hearing."

Slowly, nervous smiles break out across the room. For a moment, they speak *well* of Jesus and his fine presentation, his effective performance. Compliments to his father Joseph ("If he really *is* his father," they may have whispered to one another). Then, as if the favor of the crowd means absolutely nothing to him, Jesus proceeds to let them have a holy piece of his mind. He tells them that a hometown is a bad place for a prophet to find favor. He tells them what their questions will be (Who likes that?). In a fit of rage, the crowd drives him to the edge of a cliff, where he is miraculously left to walk away. So much for being a hometown hero.

The Spirit of God, through Jesus, proclaims good news. But the good news the Spirit brings doesn't always feel good to everyone. If you're rich and content and don't consider yourself poor, the good news ("to the poor") might not sit well with you. If you are a heart-breaker, the good news ("to bind up the broken-hearted") will call you out. If you are someone who traps people, making them captive to you and your will, the good news ("to bring freedom to the captives") will reveal your manipulation and deception.

And if you are a person who savors the favor of people and the public, then God's favor—favor that gives grace to the humble, that will resist your pride until you are shaken, trembling, and ready to let go—is a favor that may break you before it builds you.

Jesus sought only the favor of God. In a day when many of us as Christians are eager to court the favor of the culture around us, Jesus models for us that the Spirit behind the good news will give us the grace to handle the rejection, as well as the accolades, that come with the Spirit's work.

THE PRAYER

Jesus, I receive the Holy Spirit. I relinquish my need to have favor with others; I want to live a life that has favor with you. Come, Holy Spirit, show that favor to me and my congregation; awaken us to your heart of love, beating behind the good news you've given us to share. I pray in Jesus' name, amen.

THE QUESTIONS

- What does it mean to you to have the favor of God in your life?

- How does that differ from having the favor of people?

AN OLD TESTAMENT MOSAIC OF THE SPIRIT'S WORK

JOB 33:4

The Spirit of God has made me; the breath of the Almighty gives me life.

Like a glittering mosaic, the Old Testament, with its stories and passages, gives our contemporary eyes a more complete, technicolor, multi-dimensional picture of how the Holy Spirit has revealed God's presence to humanity throughout time.

As we turn toward the coming of Christ and the Spirit's work in the New Testament, let's pause to reflect briefly on what we've discovered so far.

Since the origin of the world as we know it, the Spirit of God— God's *ruakh*, God's breath, God's manifest presence—has been astoundingly creative, speaking order to chaos, form to the formless, meaning to the meaningless, all through the act of a magnificent creation. The Spirit of God sustains that good creation and all the life and activity within it, from microorganisms to trees to animals to fish to birds to ecosystems to planets, suns, supernovas, and vast galaxies. There is nothing in creation that sustains itself; the Lord created and sustains it *all*.

When God breathed into the dust of the ground, forming human-kind, male and female, to be his vice regents and image-bearers, he reflected his beauty and goodness through us in a way that sets us as the flower and crown of his good creation.[4] We engage in, and with, creation's glory, both as stewards of its treasures and appreciators of its wonders.

Within creation, the Spirit gifted human beings with skills of many kinds, to apply to the sacred activity of communion—of worship fellowship—with our covenant-forming and covenant-keeping Father. With humanity made for this bond with our Maker, a bond marked by mutual love and loyalty, a people were selected to be a kingdom of priests, a holy nation, to model for us what it means to reflect the divine image in which we are made.

The Spirit spoke through miracles, signs, and wonders to ancient Hebrew leaders who were humble, listening, obedient, and willing, often rescuing each from their own brokenness in the process and showing them abounding kindness and generosity, even when they failed.

The Spirit orchestrated individual lives and pivotal moments in salvation history to play into one mighty symphony, rushing toward the coming deliverance of the heart that would be inaugurated in the Anointed One, the Messiah. Through him, the Spirit of the Lord would bring good news of hope to the poor, to the outcast, and to the weary. The Spirit of the Lord would be on him to bring healing to the brokenhearted, to set captives free, and to lift the thick cloud of darkness that imprisons the human heart.

---

4. N. T. Wright, *Personal Interview*, Westminster Abbey, London UK, Spring 2003.

The words of Psalm 16 seem to capture the Spirit's work of guiding us: "You make known to me the path of life; you will fill me with joy in your presence, with eternal pleasures at your right hand" (Ps. 16:11).

It's exciting to see how the Spirit of God, moving in human beings over thousands of years, has always been about the same work, but in different ways—opening the heart to experience the presence and love of God, then empowering the willing disciple to live an awakened, transformed life during the years we are given. *Receive the Holy Spirit!*

THE PRAYER

Jesus, I receive the Holy Spirit. Thank you for the long story of your faithfulness, and your faithfulness to meet me, right where I am. Come, Holy Spirit, give me the strength today to live my story in connection with the plot line of your loving work throughout salvation history. I pray in Jesus' name, amen.

THE QUESTION

- As we turn our attention toward the New Testament, what ideas in today's reflection can you quickly connect with what you know about the Holy Spirit from your own learning to date?

IN THE BEGINNING, JESUS WAS THERE

JOHN 1:1–5

In the beginning was the Word, and the Word was with God, and the Word was God. He was with God in the beginning. Through him all things were made; without him nothing was made that has been made. In him was life, and that life was the light of all mankind. The light shines in the darkness, and the darkness has not overcome it.

"You had to be there."

If we've heard this once, we've heard it a hundred times. We say this when we're telling someone about an event that happened, wanting them to enter into the experience through our stellar storytelling. When it's clear we aren't communicating well enough, or the person is not connecting with the experience at the level we had hoped for, we cut our losses and say "I guess you had to be there."

But what if the person *was* there? They would simply know, like you know, how amazing the experience was. John, in the first verse of his gospel, talking about the beginning of the cosmos, is saying, *Jesus was there*. Mingling the opening words of Genesis ("In the beginning") with the Greek concept of the divine *logos* (". . . was the Word"), the apostle John makes a powerful point that has drawn many to faith in Jesus throughout the millennia.

In the beginning of creation, the Word of God, the Son of God, Jesus Christ, was *there*. And having been *there*, he knew *why* it all started, *how* it all started, and *where* it is all headed. In other words, the living Word had the Father's eternal agenda stirring in his heart as he lived and moved among us.

New creation. Out of the chaos. That's what the Trinity does. That's what the Creator did in the beginning. And that's exactly what the Word made flesh, Jesus the Son of God, came to do among us. Can I get a witness? He's doing that work in my heart as I write and it's moving me to worship; I believe he's doing it in your heart as you read. How? By the same Spirit who formed creation and who raised Jesus from the dead—the same Spirit that lives in you and me at this very moment.

Imagine John, the beloved disciple, sitting down to write his documentation of the life of Jesus. He saw the miracles. He witnessed the transfiguration. He saw Jesus alive again after his brutal crucifixion. He was present when Jesus ascended into heaven. And he was filled with the Spirit at Pentecost with everyone else, finding that God was willing to do the same kinds of miracles through him that he had done through Jesus! John has no need to inflate Jesus' story or make anything up for posterity. He's good. He's ready to write what really happened—because John *was there*.

Walking into the pages of the New Testament will reveal Jesus' most profound work, and if we could have been there at the very beginning of time, we would feel just how in concert Jesus' ministry is with the Spirit's creation work in Genesis.

With the Spirit empowering him for ministry, Jesus brings order to the chaos in the human heart, breath to spiritually dead humankind, covenant perfection in relation to the Father, signs and wonders that signal the presence of God is truly in our midst, and good news—for the poor, the captive, the prisoner—no matter our situation.

And Christ in you, through you, speaks God's loving order into the chaos of the human heart.

Let's get started in our journey with the Holy Spirit through the New Testament.

THE PRAYER

Jesus, I receive the Holy Spirit. My life is an example of you speaking your powerful word into the chaos and the disordered desires within, making me a new creation. Come, Holy Spirit, make me not only a vessel of that new creation, but a catalyst of new creation in the lives of others. I pray in Jesus' name, amen.

THE QUESTION

- Think about your own story of awakening to Christ. How has Jesus been speaking into the chaos of your life bringing his good news to transform it into something that shows off his glory?

THE HOLY SPIRIT GIVES US WHAT WE NEED FOR OBEDIENCE

LUKE 1:35

The angel answered, "The Holy Spirit will come on you, and the power of the Most High will overshadow you. So the holy one to be born will be called the Son of God."

Mary, the mother of Jesus, was a truly *awakened* leader—a receptive vessel through which the Holy Spirit could usher the Son of God into the world.

The beauty of the Scriptures is that they don't hide the real reactions of people to God's sometimes strange requests. Mary was troubled by the greeting (v. 29). She didn't know exactly what to do with the angel's words about her finding favor with God. But like her Old Testament heroes and heroines, Mary knew that "I am the Lord's servant," and "May your word to me be fulfilled" (v. 38a) would be the only appropriate response worthy of the one who called her to this unique task.

When the Holy Spirit comes to Mary, there is first an *encounter*. The Holy Spirit *happens* to Mary. Mary would conceive Jesus, of course, but we can also understand the Holy Spirit's coming on her to be a reinforcing taste of the Lord's love and presence, an encounter that will strengthen her to raise the Christ as her son over the decades ahead.

She will be faced with the harshest ridicule almost any one of us could endure, even from those who have loved her the most and the longest. She was a sweet young synagogue girl, a prize of her family, part of the youth group, and a model of devotion. What happened to her? We can imagine that Mary would frequently return, through the gift of memory, to the moment the Holy Spirit came on her—returning to that encounter for inner courage to face the less publicly affirming moments in her journey.

Second, when the Holy Spirit comes on Mary, there is *energy*. We call it *power*. Mary was spiritually tough-as-nails, a powerful, mighty soul in a tender frame, and never once do we see her falter or wander in confusion like so many of the Old Testament figures of faith who preceded her. There is good reason that Mary gets a lot of credit coming her way in the historic church—she was the first person to know who Jesus was, the first to face her fears head on with faith, and the first to give her life to seeing God's will be done through her, and through her son, no matter the cost. The Holy Spirit helped her; a deposit of spiritual energy kept her going.

Third, when the Holy Spirit comes upon Mary, there is *influence*. Obedience, a glorious first fragrance of the Spirit's work within us, takes emotional, mental, and physical resilience. God has never asked anything of anyone that didn't cost them something, even if in the end God replenished any losses incurred with even greater blessings. Mary has the capacity to do the will of God because the Spirit is continuing to influence her beyond the moment of Jesus' conception. The Spirit that overshadowed the waters at creation, is overshadowing her life.

The result? New creation. The birth of the Lord of new creation comes through a dear girl named Mary. And when it all happens, she doesn't look back.

Well done, Mary. Lead on.

THE PRAYER

Jesus, I receive the Holy Spirit. I know you may never ask of me the same kind of life-quaking obedience as you did of Mary, but I welcome you to prepare my heart to say yes to anything you desire. Come, Holy Spirit, just as you encountered, energized, and influenced Mary, do the same with me. I pray in Jesus' name, amen.

THE QUESTIONS

- Have you ever had an experience where you felt the Holy Spirit prepared you for a ministry of great importance?

- How were you prepared, and how did you experience the Spirit working through you?

THE HOLY SPIRIT WORKS THROUGH A BELOVED PERSON

MATTHEW 3:16–17

As soon as Jesus was baptized, he went up out of the water. At
that moment heaven was opened, and he saw the Spirit of God
descending like a dove and alighting on him. And a voice from heaven
said, "This is my Son, whom I love; with him I am well pleased."

Do you have a business card? I've had many through the years.
Each one typically has a few common features: my full name, my
title, my contact information, and anything else I think is special
about me that should be in the hand and mind of someone on the
receiving end.

If Jesus had a business card, it would look very different than
mine, of that I am sure. In his baptismal waters, the Holy Spirit
descends. The Son of God sees the Spirit descending on him. And
the Father's voice speaks Jesus' business card out into the world for
all to hear.

This is my Son. Jesus receives a word of *identity*. He is seen, known,
and loved for who and whose he is. He belongs to Someone, his

Father. He will know his place in the world no matter what resistance or opportunities to feel misplaced or misfit may come. He is prepared to be unloved by the crowds because the Father has settled the love question before he even begins his ministry.

Whom I love. Jesus receives a word of *affection*. He will face large crowds, all shouting his name, both in a spirit of overwhelming appreciation and in a spirit of utter rejection. He will know he is loved before all that begins. He will not need to court the crowd for his sense of belovedness. Neither their accolades nor the accusations will move him.

With him I am well pleased. Jesus receives a word of *affirmation*. Jesus has not done one miracle by the time of his baptism. He does not need to have succeeded, or to have accomplished something, for his Father to approve of him. "Jesus," it seems the Father is saying, "I approve of you if you never do even one thing." That is what love does; it removes our need to achieve to be affirmed.

Jesus' business card would have had one word on it: *Son.* And that word would capture his sense of identity, his sense of belovedness, and his sense of approval. If my own son had a business card that only had that one word beneath his name, I would be the proudest father on earth. What's on your spiritual business card? What if it was only your name, and "son" or "daughter" beneath it?

When the foundation for the Spirit's power to work through us in spiritual gifts is love, we will represent the Father's heart as we do the business to which he's invited us. We won't be seeking identity, affection, or approval from fickle crowds.

To first know our belovedness is the only way to live like Jesus in this world. And the Spirit confers the love of the Father to our hearts.

Jesus, I receive the Holy Spirit. Just as you found your identity in the love of the Father for you, so I too want to find my identity in the Father's love for me. Come, Holy Spirit, let my life be marked by belovedness, so when your power works through me I can keep it all in perspective. I pray in Jesus' name, amen.

THE QUESTIONS

- Do you have a sense of the love of the Father naming you, loving you, and affirming you as you begin today?

- What could you do to reclaim that reality in your heart?

THE HOLY SPIRIT GIVES NEW BIRTH

JOHN 3:5–8

Jesus answered, "Very truly I tell you, no one can enter the kingdom of God unless they are born of water and the Spirit. Flesh gives birth to flesh, but the Spirit gives birth to spirit. You should not be surprised at my saying, 'You must be born again.' The wind blows wherever it pleases. You hear its sound, but you cannot tell where it comes from or where it is going. So it is with everyone born of the Spirit."

I had the privilege of being present for the birth of each of our three children. While the birth of each child was unique, and each birth process had its challenges and blessings, there is one experience that was consistent in all three cases—when we looked into the eyes of our baby, our hearts were full of utter delight. The innocence, dependence, and "take it all in" gleam in a baby's eyes is so profound, isn't it? Love overtakes us. The biblical phrase "new creation" takes on a whole new meaning.

The Father took delight when we were born into the world. We were beloved before we even made a sound. And when we were born again, that delight must have gone to another level. Jesus says to Nicodemus that a person must be "born of water and the Spirit" to enter into the fullness of the kingdom of God.

While scholars have been writing books about the mysteries swirling in this passage for millennia, being "born of the Spirit" remains a living reality for the awakened heart. We were one type of person—thinking, feeling, and acting one way—and then we met Jesus. We believed. Our eyes were opened. Something happened, and began to happen in our hearts; we re-came into the world a new creation.

What happened? The Holy Spirit was now living in us. Like the wind Jesus describes in our opening passage, we didn't see it coming. We didn't always know where the Holy Spirit was taking us along the way. But we trusted the wind of God's Spirit. We had a wonderful counselor at work within our spirits, opening us up to God's love (Rom. 5:5) and guiding us into new life (John 16:13).

We had become, truly, a new creation in Christ, starting fresh with eyes wide open, taking it all in as even the world around us seemed to become new. We began to learn that moving with the Holy Spirit is more like a dance than a hike. He leads us, and he guides us, often into the same places our feet have been before. And we see those places with new vision!

I have a friend who was caught up in many of the dark things this world has to offer. On the day he came to faith in Jesus, the only words I could use to describe the transformation were "new birth." He was hard and hateful one moment, and in the next (with a journey of discipleship and maturation in faith ahead), he had the innocence of a newborn babe sparkling in his eyes. Jesus' love met him. Jesus' love transformed him. And Jesus' love gave him new birth.

Many of us have witnessed this new-beginning-transformation again and again, and I am eager to see that work of transformation continue until I am conformed to Christ. Second Corinthians 5:17 says, "Therefore, if anyone is in Christ, the new creation has come:

The old has gone, the new is here!" First Peter 1:3 says, "Praise be to the God and Father of our Lord Jesus Christ! In his great mercy he has given us new birth into a living hope through the resurrection of Jesus Christ from the dead." Thank you, Lord, for new creation life! Thank you, Lord, for a new and living hope!

THE PRAYER

Jesus, I receive the Holy Spirit. Let the maturing work you began as I awoke to new life, a new creation, a twice-born follower, continue until I become like Jesus. Come, Holy Spirit, work in me, from the inside out, into new ways of seeing and understanding the world around me. I pray in Jesus' name, amen.

THE QUESTIONS

- Was there a moment, or a period of time, to which you could point when you were born again by the Spirit?

- If so, what was that season like, and how is the maturing process going?

THE HOLY SPIRIT IS WITH YOU AND IN YOU

JOHN 14:16–17

"And I will ask the Father, and he will give you another advocate
to help you and be with you forever—the Spirit of truth. The world
cannot accept him, because it neither sees him nor knows him.
But you know him, for he lives with you and will be in you."

Do you have any helpers in your life? You know, the kind of people who seem to be available, right when you need them, for some errand, some support, some time, or some strength that helps you move forward on any given day? Have you ever experienced a moment when you needed them, or someone, to be available and they simply could not be available for some reason? It's hard; people are limited beings, making their ability to help limited as well.

To receive the Holy Spirit, is to receive the divine *Helper*—a permanent, indwelling advocate, encourager, guide, and support—to live and move within our hearts in even the loneliest of times. In one of the most famous Holy Spirit passages in the Scriptures, Jesus tells his disciples that they will receive a helper, an advocate, a *parakletos*—a Paraclete—one who will help them walk the journey of covenant faith, make Christlike decisions, and draw on the power of the Holy Spirit from within. The Helper will be available to them at *all* times. The Helper is unlimited in presence and resource.

Let's back up to take a peek into the emotional state of the disciples when Jesus shares the words in today's text, taking a guess at some of their inner responses to what is occurring in front of them. In John 13, Jesus washes his disciples' feet. "Hmm. Interesting." He predicts a betrayal. "Ouch. That's not good. That's really not good, Jesus." Then he tells Peter that he will deny him three times. "Gulp" (that one belongs only to Peter). Anxiety.

Then, chapter 14 begins with Jesus telling them their hearts shouldn't be troubled. A storm is brewing, and they can sense it coming. Then he speaks to them of the Father's house, and that he is going to prepare a place for them. *Wait.* Going? Going where? "I will come to take you to be with me. You know the way to the place where I am going" (v. 3b–4). Wait. What? You're leaving? This is a very bad time to be using leaving language, Jesus.

That's when Jesus speaks to the orphan-spirit: that brooding, hollowing, I'll-be-left-alone loneliness that is overtaking his disciples. And he longs for them to feel the closeness of the Father that he feels. Enter the Holy Spirit. "I will ask the Father," Jesus says, and the Helper of the fearful, powerless heart will come. He will be "*with* you and will be *in* you."

I, too, have often longed for Jesus to be alive and present, right here in front of me. Jesus was clear in John 16:7, "But very truly I tell you, it is for your good that I am going away. Unless I go away, the Advocate will not come to you; but if I go, I will send him to you."

Today, if you've known that loneliness, that longing, take the comfort Jesus was offering to his disciples, that is now fulfilled among us. The Helper is *here*. The Spirit is in you; guiding your heart and mind to truth. Convicting you of areas in your life in which you are missing the mark and missing his heart for you. Revealing your new name as a child of God. Showing you what to do next, where the Father is at work, and how to partner with him in the awakening of other hearts to wholeness and healing.

We are the people in whom he dwells, and the mystery of the gospel is Christ in us, "the hope of glory" (Col. 1:26–27). "I will not leave you as orphans; I will come to you. Before long, the world will not see me anymore, but you will see me. Because I live, you also will live" (John 14:18–19). The Holy Spirit helps us in our times of need; we are never, ever alone.

THE PRAYER

Jesus, I receive the Holy Spirit. I have known times and places where I felt left alone; and there you were, closer to me than anyone ever could be. Come, Holy Spirit, in worship I draw near to you and become aware of your presence; I put my trust in you. I pray in Jesus' name, amen.

THE QUESTIONS

- What helps you become aware of the Helper living with you and within you?

- Share your thoughts with someone else and ask, "Do you have any ideas for how I could make these practices a more frequent part of my day and week?"

THE HOLY SPIRIT REVEALS JESUS

JOHN 15:26

"When the Advocate comes, whom I will send to you from the Father—the Spirit of truth who goes out from the Father—he will testify about me."

Saying the Nicene Creed is one of my favorite things to do. I mean it. Every morning I sit down in my prayer chair (I call it that because prayer and worship are what happen most frequently while I am sitting on that piece of furniture). As part of my daily regimen, I recite or sing a few choice pieces that align my heart to faith and trust. The Nicene Creed is one of those.

In that creed, the wording highlights what is said about the Holy Spirit in John 15:26. In describing the Holy Spirit, the Nicene Creed says "We believe in the Holy Spirit, the Lord, the giver of life, who proceeds . . ." Theologians have wrestled with the ideas around this part of the creed for a long time, and historic theological wranglings are not our focus for today.

What I am interested in, and what I think we should all be interested in, is that the Spirit is *sent* to us "from the Father," and "goes out from the Father" according to this little verse in John. In other words, the Spirit comes to us from the very heart—the loving, essential nature—of the Father. When something or Someone is sent, there is always an intended recipient.

The follower of Jesus is that recipient.

This beautiful chapter begins with Jesus using the metaphor of vines and branches to emphasize our union with him, as well as the Father's work of tending this sacred garden of relationship. Terms like *remaining, abiding, pruning, fruit,* and other words emerge to anchor us, establish us, settle us, and clarify for us what it means to remain in the love of Jesus . . . remain in the love of the Father . . . and remain in the love of one another.

Then, Jesus gives the challenge that follows the encouragement. He reminds them that the world will hate them, and they should see that as par for the course when following Jesus and doing the work of the Father. Their job is not to provoke that hatred unnecessarily by acting strange for strangeness' sake; rather, they will be seen as strange, and hated, because of the way they choose to be human in the world.

Through all of their abiding, trials, and troubles, according to the last phrase, the Spirit will do a very particular job—in you and through you. The Spirit of truth will testify about, witness to, tell the story—of Jesus. Again and again.

Jesus is the Way as we know (John 14:6). He is also the Life. But in the middle of it all, in the middle of the hard choosing of the *way* that leads to *life*, we'll need the Spirit of *truth* to keep us on track. Jesus is the Truth that sets us free from our broken thinking and feeling on a daily basis (John 8:31–32).

The Spirit, all along the way, will continue to reveal Jesus. If Jesus is being hidden, obscured, mocked, or diminished, the Spirit is not behind it. Shake it off. The Spirit reveals who Jesus is, what he is for, and why he does what he does. The Spirit helps us understand the reasons behind the hard work of transformation going on in our lives. The Spirit keeps us living in union, in abiding love, with Jesus.

The Holy Spirit, sent from the Father, reveals Jesus.

THE QUESTIONS

- Have you ever testified to someone about Jesus, telling your story and inviting them into the same kind of awakening that you experienced?

- Is there someone you are praying for right now, a friend, family member, or neighbor who is ready for the Spirit to testify about Jesus through you?

THE HOLY SPIRIT GUIDES US INTO ALL TRUTH

JOHN 16:13

"But when he, the Spirit of truth, comes, he will guide you into all the truth. He will not speak on his own; he will speak only what he hears, and he will tell you what is yet to come."

One of the greatest leadership lessons I ever learned was to treat communication with others as a collaboration, rather than as a one-way enterprise. Sometimes we need to restate something in a conversation, reading the eyes of the person to whom we are speaking, to help both of us unpack a meaning we don't want to miss.

In John 16:13, a verse very similar to John's earlier words in John 15:26 appears. In the earlier verse, Jesus, explaining the work of the Holy Spirit, says, "he will testify about me." Now, a bit later, Jesus restates a similar idea, but with a slight twist: "he will guide you into all the truth." He follows this up with a further, more detailed description: "he will speak only what he hears, and he will tell you what is yet to come." Jesus then clarifies even further in verses 14–15: "He will glorify me because it is from me that he will receive what he will make known to you. All that belongs to the Father is mine. That is why I said the Spirit will receive from me what he will make known to you."

I don't know about you, but I need some Holy Spirit guidance in this lifetime. Since I was a young man, I have actively gathered wisdom for key decisions from family members, mentors, friends, coworkers, pastors, and a network of acquaintances. All my sources offer valuable input when I ask for it (and sometimes when I don't). In many cases, those I ask seek to guide me toward "whatever is true, whatever is noble, whatever is right, whatever is pure, whatever is lovely, whatever is admirable . . . excellent or praiseworthy" (Phil. 4:8). But their perspective is limited, and I still have to discern the best course of action on a big decision before the Lord.

This is why it is so important to cultivate our ability to discern, to perceive, what the Holy Spirit "who guides us into all the truth" is saying—as it may be in contrast to what others might be saying! Instead of learning to discern and listen to the voice of the Holy Spirit, many of us immediately draw on those around us, our experiences, best practices, or even what we have learned in corporate or church worlds.

We waffle and struggle, because both our sources and we have limited understanding. We may try to call that spiritual discernment, but it's not the same thing. Experience is helpful, but what if Jesus, speaking by the Spirit within you, has something to ask of you that contradicts those experiences, best practices, and contextual learning environments? Remember Peter and the vision of the unclean animals (Acts 10:9–23)? Remember Paul and the man from Macedonia (Acts 16:9–10)? Our best thinking is not always . . . best.

Discernment comes by cultivating a listening life to the Holy Spirit. We wisely take in all the information on a decision, weighing the pros and cons of the various directions we might take. We soak in the Scriptures and live a life yielded to God. But then we offer to God what Ignatius of Loyola called our "attachments"[5]—preferred outcomes (even good ones) we are clinging to inwardly that may get in the way of hearing the Holy Spirit speak to us. We name our preferred outcomes, and lay them out on the altar, saying "Father, your will be done; I desire only to do your will." At this point, our hearts are ready to perceive God's peace, or what Ignatius called "consolation," about a decision.

The Holy Spirit is going to speak to us the heart of Jesus. Learning to pause and discern God's desires for a course of action must become part of the Spirit-led leader's toolkit and the toolkit of the Christian (Rom. 8:14). Truth is not easily found in a world where falsehoods and personal preferences are often more intriguing. The Holy Spirit helps us become captivated by truth, for the purpose of revealing Jesus in the world.

THE PRAYER

Jesus, I receive the Holy Spirit. Teach me to discern your voice of truth speaking through the noise of my daily life. Come, Holy Spirit, teach me to lay down my own wisdom to begin to access the wisdom of heaven. I pray in Jesus' name, amen.

THE QUESTIONS

- Do you have a process by which you make decisions?

- What have you learned about following the Holy Spirit's promptings from a few decisions you have made?

---

5. The idea of attachments comes from the Spiritual Exercises of Ignatius of Loyola, and is an important idea in Ignatian spirituality.

THE HOLY SPIRIT GLORIFIES JESUS

JOHN 16:14–15; 17:23

"He [the Spirit] will glorify me because it is from me that he will receive what he will make known to you. All that belongs to the Father is mine. That is why I said the Spirit will receive from me what he will make known to you. . . .

"I in them and you in me—so that they may be brought to complete unity. Then the world will know that you sent me and have loved them even as you have loved me."

We're dropping in on a long conversation that Jesus is having with his disciples in John 14–17. This potent section in John's gospel even includes a precious prayer (John 17), straight from the heart of Jesus to his Father—a prayer for the disciples and for us. What a gift to every generation of the saints.

In the display verses, we see that the Father has sent the Spirit to reveal and to glorify Jesus. The Spirit is the divine interpreter given to us to live within and to make Jesus glorious to us. And, ultimately, the Spirit will do the work of making Jesus glorious to the world. Pause. Take that in.

Over and over Jesus is communicating that union between the Father and Son, and between us and one another (John 17:11), are the greatest spiritual wins we could imagine in this lifetime.

It is the Spirit that keeps this goodness of relationship sustained and growing between us all: "I in them and you in me—so that they may be brought to complete unity. Then the world will know that you sent me and have loved them even as you have loved me" (John 17:23).

In other words, our love, our union with the Father and the Son, reinforced by the sealing touch of the Holy Spirit binding our hearts together, is what is to overflow to touch the world. The world is in a truth struggle right now. Many are no longer sure what to believe, what is credible, and what is the right way to think about the world. Jesus is providing a next step for us, a way forward, to revealing the gospel in our homes, churches, and cities. What is the next step?

It is to focus on our union with him. Yes, we can lament our lack of unity in the church. Yes, we can work toward maintaining peace with one another. But if we focus on union with Jesus, the Spirit will glorify him in the world. Intimacy is the prerequisite to unity. That spiritual math will always remain the same. And the truth is, cultivating intimacy with the Father, a vibrant life of yielded relationship that holds no part of ourselves off limits to his loving input and transformation, is harder than messing with the knobs of unity in the church.

What keeps us in union with the Lord? *Worship*—its Scriptures, its music, its prayers, its creeds, its life, keeps us loving and receiving love. Doing what Jesus did and called us to do will also keep our union with Christ growing—preaching good news to the poor, binding up the wounds of the brokenhearted, serving one another in love, embodying the fruits of the Holy Spirit—love, joy, peace, patience, kindness, goodness, faithfulness, gentleness, and self-control. Maintaining sustaining friendships that point us to Christ, like discipleship bands, will keep us walking in union with Jesus.

All these things will reinforce our union with Christ, in heart, in mind, in body, in disposition, in instinct, in thought, in word, in deed—in love. That union will help us "maintain the unity of the Spirit in the bond of peace" (Eph. 4:3).

The Spirit will then glorify Jesus in our eyes—and in the eyes of the world.

THE PRAYER

Jesus, I receive the Holy Spirit. I desire to receive what you would communicate to me by your Holy Spirit within. Come, Holy Spirit, show me today what my part is in nurturing the union you began with me, and the riches of your heart that are available to me. I pray in Jesus' name, amen.

THE QUESTION

- Quiet your heart in a posture of receptivity. Ask the Holy Spirit to show you one thing you can regularly do to reinforce your union with Christ. Write down what he shows you, and commit to it for at least one week. After one week ask yourself, "How did it go?"

THE HOLY SPIRIT REVEALS TO US THE DEEP THINGS OF GOD

1 CORINTHIANS 2:9–10

However, as it is written: "What no eye has seen, what no ear has heard, and what no human mind has conceived"— the things God has prepared for those who love him—these are the things God has revealed to us by his Spirit.

The Spirit searches all things, even the deep things of God.

My grandfather had the spiritual gift of wisdom (1 Cor. 12:8). He came to faith in Jesus later in life, and when he was in his final years and his heart was failing him, I would sit with him on his front porch swing as he shared wisdom with his teenage grandson. In retrospect, there were times, as he came closer to death, his wisdom seemed otherworldly.

The Spirit living in him was revealing to him the "deep things of God." He was seeing beyond the reach of his physical eyes as the Spirit opened the eyes of his heart to the waiting world ahead. The Spirit stirred in him a longing for a world he could not yet see, but that he could taste in his spirit—and wanted more than life here could offer him. In that desire, he was inducted into a community of heroes and heroines of faith who "Were longing for a better country—a heavenly one. Therefore God is not ashamed to be called their God, for he has prepared a city for them" (Heb. 11:16).

That longing within us is Spirit-born, and gives us a unique, and often countercultural, perspective on things. The Spirit of God is the Spirit of Revelation. We are invited to understand what God understands, and this has always proven to be a great gift to Christians, and to the church. Such wisdom has often made us look silly to the world and its vision of the good life.

In verses 3–5, Paul tells the Corinthians how his words lacked eloquence and were not seasoned with choice morsels from the Twitter feeds of his day. He tells the believers he came with weakness, fear, and trembling. Clearly, he was not out to impress them into embracing the gospel (pause, reflect on contemporary Christian subculture, repeat). He also tells them that he came with a "demonstration of the Spirit's power"—evidencing God's power in a way that was impossible to replicate.

Our words can sound similar to the world's words. Our actions can sometimes look similar to the world's actions. But the Spirit's power? It is inimitable. Paul knew that the wisdom of this world is confounded by the Spirit's power. That power can be evidenced in signs and wonders, or in our unique wisdom—our perspective— on this life. Note this: it is not our words that will ultimately persuade this generation; a demonstration of the Spirit's power will fit the job description we are now filling with words.

The Spirit knows the depths, the immensity, the grandeur of the world to which we are heading. And the Spirit stirs in our hearts a longing for it, like one magnet is drawn to another. We are being spiritually pulled, by Christ's transforming love, toward our home, a world we have yet to see. A world that is creating longing within us.

And what emerges from that longing? The wisdom of God. We perceive and speak of another world, another way of being human, another vision of our preferred future—and it powers our souls with a hope that refuses the best this world has to offer.

THE PRAYER

Jesus, I receive the Holy Spirit. There is a longing in my heart, that you have put there, to see the new creation you have planned come to full fruition. Come, Holy Spirit, help me speak, influence, and minister out of that longing, in the wisdom that comes from you. I pray in Jesus' name, amen.

THE QUESTION

- What kind of "world to come" longings has the Holy Spirit put in your heart?

THE HOLY SPIRIT IS A BODY BUILDER

1 CORINTHIANS 12:12–14

Just as a body, though one, has many parts, but all its many parts form one body, so it is with Christ. For we were all baptized by one Spirit so as to form one body—whether Jews or Gentiles, slave or free—and we were all given the one Spirit to drink. Even so the body is not made up of one part but of many.

How many churches are in the world today? That question may be a bit beyond the scope of our immediate trivia knowledge. Let's try another question. How many Churches are there in the world today? See what I did there? A capital "C" puts the question in an entirely different category. There is only one church, only one body of Christ, according to the Scriptures. Jesus alone knows who is in his church. The parable of the sheep and the goats is a parable for our time, but at the end of the day, there is only one flock of sheep. And Jesus knows each sheep by name (John 10:3).

The Holy Spirit, in 1 Corinthians 12:12–14, communicates to us that if we were baptized by one Holy Spirit, then we are a part of the one body of Christ. We all drink the water of God's love and power at the same fountain. Like little children on the playground, we may try to push one another away to get our turn, hog the fountain, or put our claim on it. But there is plenty for everyone, and, if you look around, there are many fountains at which to drink the same living water.

The Holy Spirit is all about making—bringing together—the body of Christ. We are one body, but there are many parts taking their place to embody Jesus' life and ministry in their unique locales and neighborhoods across the planet. When we start complaining about the rest of the church, or if we even lose ourselves in a whine-fest complaining in sweeping terms about how broken we as the church are, I believe we have stepped over a very important line.

First of all, when we complain about the church as a whole, that is just a sorry, weak, lazy, and distorted replacement for biblical lament. We are welcomed to lament, to grieve, and to pray for the body of Christ when seeming fractures and relational puzzles emerge. But it seems that God's Word gives us no quarter to stand as judge and jury over what is happening with our brothers and sisters in different parts of the body.

Secondly, when we stage a whine-fest complaining in sweeping terms about how broken we are as the church, it is like declaring: "I know all and see all, and this body is a mess. It's a hot mess, I tell you." At that point, we are on the wrong side of God. Do we really think the gates of hell are prevailing against the church, even when Jesus said they would not (Matt. 16:18)? No, they are not. Times are hard, yes. But the Spirit sees the true, robust, and unconquerable body of Jesus rising with him toward the day new creation's dawn breaks on the earth. Full stop. The body of Christ is beautiful, and strong, and always the Beloved of Jesus.

The Holy Spirit is a body builder, and that is who we are to become as well if the Spirit lives in us. If we spend our time lost in complaint, we are spending our energies in the opposite direction in which the Spirit is spending the Spirit's energies. Jesus is about building his church, and the gates of hell will not topple it, divide it, or diffuse its power.

Let's turn our energies to pray for the body of Christ in all its local forms to learn what it means to live in union with the Father and the Son once more. Then, let's pray for the unity that flows out of that intimacy. It is the Holy Spirit who gives us the capacity for unity in a fallen world. The body of Christ is designed to be a sign, a wonder, a declaration that unity can occur in any age.

THE PRAYER

Jesus, I receive the Holy Spirit. Forgive me if I have become discouraged about the state of your church and spoken ill of your body; I don't see all, and I repent. Come, Holy Spirit, turn the lament and grief in my heart to praise and prayer for your kingdom to come in the beautiful body of Christ. I pray in Jesus' name, amen.

THE QUESTION

- What good, right, and lovely things do you see happening in and through the church across the world?

THE HOLY SPIRIT EMPOWERS US WITH THE FATHER'S LOVE

ROMANS 8:14–15

For those who are led by the Spirit of God are the children of God. The Spirit you received does not make you slaves, so that you live in fear again; rather, the Spirit you received brought about your adoption to sonship. And by him we cry, "Abba, Father."

I've been fascinated over the last few decades with how often power is viewed as the big idea behind spiritual gifts—rather than the more foundational, bigger idea of love. The Holy Spirit of God is first about the work of *loving a soul to awakening*; the expressions of spiritual power that flow from that love and compassion are the overflow of the love that moves the Father in heaven.

So why do we fixate primarily on power when we talk about the Spirit? Humans can get overly excited about spectacles and miracles, like those who asked Jesus for signs, forgetting what is motivating that wonder and giving it meaning. God's power is loving power. Anything that flows from God's hand to us is touched and shaped by his love.

In this passage we see that the Father's love is always making his power benevolent—the Spirit sets us free (2 Cor. 3:17) and brings us deeper into love. Sabbath, for example, is all about deepening in love as we refuse to be a slave to work and reorient our identity once again to simply being a beloved child of our Abba in heaven. We are made for the Father's perfect love, no longer to be subject to the bonds of spiritual, psychological, or emotional slavery (Gal. 5:1).

As someone who has spent the last decades of my life in church contexts that embrace the gifts the Holy Spirit gives, from what we might call natural gifts (teaching, administration) all the way to the momentary or ongoing charisms (healing and prophecy), I have at times seen a fixation on an experience of power and spectacle as the goal. When a limb is healed right there on the spot, it's exciting! When blindness is healed and a person sees for the first time in years, it's wonderful!

But the healing is not the point of what is happening in that moment. It never is. The love of God for the person is the most amazing thing happening in that moment. When someone's eyes light up with the love of God, expressed in quiet tears or loud rejoicing at what God has done, I'm pretty sure the angels in heaven are dancing—whether a miracle occurs or not!

I am so grateful for those who mentored me in praying for the sick and those in need. Those men and women would always remind me that the very least a person should leave with after a time of me praying for them is a deeper experience of the love of God. When a person feels that Jesus sees them, and knows them, it can trigger a deep inner healing to which even a physical healing can seem secondary. God's love brings an eternal miracle of union with the person. That is always the Father's goal.

Keeping the Father's love as the goal of every time of praying for someone, we won't get hung up on whether our prayers for them worked or not. We will stay focused on God's love for the person as we pray. That focus will cause us to be sensitive in our praying, rather than distracted by a fix-it mentality, or overly dramatic attempts to work up emotion. That same focus will also help us keep our distance from cynicism when someone is not healed through our participation with the Father in praying for them.

Becoming like a child to our Abba God is a prerequisite for kingdom flourishing. The Holy Spirit releases us from fear into loving dependence on our Creator. Whether we are the one praying for someone, or the one being prayed for, a continual reminder that we are loved by God truly casts out fear (1 John 4:18).

A loved person is a force to be reckoned with; just like Jesus before us.

THE PRAYER

Jesus, I receive the Holy Spirit. I want to participate in others experiencing the love of the Father through whatever gifts of the Spirit flow through me. Come, Holy Spirit, use me in my natural gifts and in more momentary or ongoing gifts, to participate with in you awakening hearts to your love. I pray in Jesus' name, amen.

THE QUESTIONS

- Is there someone you could pray for this week who is in need of an experience of the Father's love?

- What would happen if you asked if you could pray for them, and you started off praying for the Father's love to fill them?

THE HOLY SPIRIT TEACHES US WHAT TO SAY

LUKE 12:11–12

"When you are brought before synagogues, rulers and authorities, do not worry about how you will defend yourselves or what you will say, for the Holy Spirit will teach you at that time what you should say."

When we think about what it means to receive the Holy Spirit, we may be quick to think of God's affection filling us (love), or God's spiritual gifts operating through us (power). Both of these are vital aspects of the way the Holy Spirit works in and through us. Yet by taking our time, wandering with a discoverer's eye through Old and New Testament revelations of God's presence, we're gaining a more fully-scoped vision of the person and work of the Holy Spirit. This will serve us as we follow Jesus in the love and power of the Holy Spirit today.

So what does Luke 12:11–12 teach us about the Holy Spirit?

Luke 12:11–12 is, in my view, a Holy Spirit word about *inspiration* (and its archnemesis, *worry;* but we'll talk about that in a moment). Inspiration literally means to be "in-spirited," or "breathed into." It's what happens when we, like the sail of a boat being filled with the wind, are *in-spirited* and moved by the Holy Spirit to do something, say something, or be something the moment requires.

In this passage, Jesus is speaking to his disciples about scary, safety-threatening situations they might find themselves in because of their faith. Those that can harm your body, or even shame or imprison you, according to the Lord of heaven and earth, are not to be feared. But still, he knows we will fear because we don't see the future—we don't know the outcome as we stand before the powers of this world that may prove to be merciless. In other words, we will always be tempted to *worry*.

Jesus is saying that one can choose not to give worry its sway ("Do not worry"), and that the Holy Spirit will do the teaching, and ultimately, the talking when we are called to give an account for our faith. As a professional and card-carrying worrier most of my life, I've had to disown that unholy identity as I've walked with Jesus.

Jesus doesn't worry. Jesus in me doesn't worry. So I choose not to worry, and I am still learning how to put worry in the back seat even when it is always begging me to drive. I am learning to see it, name it, address it when it rears its head, and to let faith take the lead. To worry is to believe that God's future is less real than the distorted future my mind is constructing. The people of God are not designed for worry. Worry will make us sick. The people of God are designed for faith. Faith will make us healthy.

Returning to our sailboat analogy, worry ties up our sail and keeps it twisted down tight so it can't open up to catch the wind of inspiration. But when worry is ousted from our boat, we can then open up to God's presence, even in turbulence, to be filled with inspiration in our moment of need.

The Holy Spirit is with us when we have time to plan what we need to say, whether we are giving an account of our faith behind a pulpit, on the front lawn with our neighbor, or in preparation to stand before a tribunal. Many brothers and sisters around the world are in this latter situation. Let's pray for them. The Holy Spirit will also be with us, inspiring us, when any situation demands we give an extemporaneous articulation of our faith in Christ.

Either way, we as Christians are called to resist worry and its choking bonds. We are called to keep our sails open to the inspiration of the Holy Spirit. The Spirit will help us know what to say, what to do, in our time of need.

THE PRAYER

Jesus, I receive the Holy Spirit. I may have spent years practicing worry, but I want to spend the next years displacing worry in my life with faith. Come, Holy Spirit, empower me to live beyond worry and to rely on your inspiration in the challenging moments of today. I pray in Jesus' name, amen.

THE QUESTIONS

- Have you ever been in a situation where you believe the Holy Spirit gave you the words to speak, even when you had not planned what you were going to say?

- What happened as a result?

WALKING BY THE SPIRIT LEADS TO LIFE

GALATIANS 5:16–18

So I say, walk by the Spirit, and you will not gratify the desires
of the flesh. For the flesh desires what is contrary to the Spirit,
and the Spirit what is contrary to the flesh. They are in conflict
with each other, so that you are not to do whatever you want.
But if you are led by the Spirit, you are not under the law.

Near our home is a walking path encircling a large field. The path
is paved, with signs that give you a sense that the trail has been
curated to fulfill a particular purpose. It's flat and wide enough
for various activities, so it's perfect for walkers, runners, joggers,
roamers, shufflers, cyclists, hoppers, and skippers. It also happens
to work well for families pushing strollers, large groups of teenagers, and seniors.

No one (at least that I know of) judges you on that path; once I
walked about two miles an hour after a major surgery and everyone
passed me with a smile and a glance of compassion. There are rest
stops along the way and markers that let you know you're still
headed in the right direction. The path *works*, rain or shine. It's not
overgrown; it is clearly tended to on a regular basis.

But the field it surrounds? It is wild, rarely mowed, and full of high grasses, hidden holes, thorny weeds, and critters of various kinds. When it rains, we could lose someone in there. The mud, mixed with the wild growth, would be debilitating and disorienting. To walk across the field is certainly an option; it's wide enough for incredibly large groups, even whole towns of people (get it?), but if you choose that way you may arrive on the other side with a broken ankle, a dozen bug bites, or worse. But if you want to walk that path, you can.

Walking by the Spirit is like choosing the curated path. The Spirit knows the way. Jesus and the saints have blazed the trail. The Spirit tends to and defines the path to life (Ps. 16:11). The Spirit leads on that path so that you and I end up achieving the goals for which the path was designed—and we were made. The Spirit leads us into truth (John 16:13), yields in us the fruits of love, joy, peace, patience, kindness, goodness, faithfulness, gentleness, and self-control (Gal. 5:22–23), and fills us with power (Acts 1:8) to live as followers of Jesus.

However, the wide path across the field (Matt. 7:13) is an option. And the Lord allows us the opportunity to learn from ill-chosen journeys along that path by dealing with the consequences of our choice.

Gratifying ourselves in the context of Galatians 5:16–18 could be understood as *indulging* ourselves. When we indulge ourselves—our bodies, our minds, our emotions, our senses—we get too much of a good thing and we can lose our way in the wild. Choices that seemed so pleasurable, so satisfying in the moment end up taking us places that lead to a long, slow death.

When we accompany the Spirit on the path of life, the Spirit shows us the way that leads us to the human flourishing we so deeply desire. As we are led, we are free to express passion and engage restraint, to embrace freedom (Gal. 5:1), and to welcome limitations.

All this the Spirit affirms—speaking to us through God's Word, speaking to us through others and their testimonies of faith, and speaking to us in our hearts as the indwelling Shepherd leading us home. To walk by the Spirit means we choose the path that Jesus walked ahead of us—his Spirit within us knows that path well.

THE PRAYER

Jesus, I receive the Holy Spirit. I am learning to follow your lead through your Word, through the insights of others who have gone before me, and through cultivating intimacy with you in the secret place. Come, Holy Spirit, keep me on the narrow path that leads to life. I choose to walk with you. I pray in Jesus' name, amen.

THE QUESTION

- What is your own testimony about how you ended up on the path to life?

THE HOLY SPIRIT BRINGS FREEDOM

2 CORINTHIANS 3:17

Now the Lord is the Spirit, and where the Spirit
of the Lord is, there is freedom.

I remember the moment like it was yesterday. The young woman sat in front of our group, sharing her testimony. We all have a story—one in which Jesus steps into the room, looks us in the eye, and invites us to a new life. That's what happened with her. But the room Jesus walks into is different for all of us, and the one she was in was darker than any I had heard of before.

In short, she had lost her way as a teenager and ended up addicted to drugs and alcohol. She did anything she could to get the money she needed to anaesthetize the deep pain within her. Ending up in the dark world of prostitution, she was broken, confused, and full of inner and outer chaos. She prayed in the only way she knew how—*desperation*.

The Holy Spirit entered the room of her despair.

Divinely orchestrated events led a group of followers of Jesus to find her and to welcome her to a new life. She said yes and never looked back. That day, face beaming, she told her story while tears streamed down her face. She shared how clean, how pure, and how loved she felt by her Father in heaven. She was the bride of Christ. Who could take this new life from her? No one. No one had the power to remove the love from her heart that was overflowing in gratitude as she spoke. Her life, completely turned around, was now spent reaching out to other young women caught in the same cycle of desperation.

As I sat there listening, tears streamed down my face as well. I remember thinking this thought so clearly: *No therapist, no celebrity, no community, even no family, on their own, could bring about the kind of utter transformation I am seeing in front of me. Her life has truly been made new. She is a new creation, a sign and a wonder and a declaration that Jesus loves and has the power to heal.*

Freedom is a word that can be used to mean many things these days. I can be free to do what I want. I can also be free to do what God wants. In the former case, I am my guide, and while I may not end up in a room like anyone else, I seem to be pretty good at creating my own problems. In the latter case, freedom means what it did to the woman at the well—I am free to choose Jesus as my guide, to follow his path to hope, and to surrender myself to a Father who loves me so much he will use any situation to bind my heart in greater union with his.

The Spirit of the Lord is right here, right now, ready to bring freedom to you. Whatever the awakening is that is your next step, say yes to open eyes and a Spirit-filling that will give what you need to step through this season into the new that Jesus has for you.

And if you know of someone who is locked in a room of their own or another's making, hidden away so that only those who are closest to them can see how afraid or lost they truly are, pause and pray with me for the true Spirit of Freedom to shake the foundations of their prison (Acts 16:25–26) and to break the chains that that have kept them bound within.

Where the Spirit of the Lord is, there is *freedom*.

THE PRAYER

Jesus, I receive the Holy Spirit. I feel the power of your presence with me once again, reminding me how far we've come and how much you have done in my life. Come, Holy Spirit, give me hope for my own wholeness, and use me to intercede in the lives of others who need to taste the extent of the freedom only you can give. I pray in Jesus' name, amen.

THE QUESTIONS

- Is there someone that comes to mind that you could spend the week offering to God in prayer?

- Invite the Holy Spirit to break in, once again, and believe that the Lord will bring them to his freedom.

THE FRUIT OF THE SPIRIT CAN BURST FROM YOUR LIFE

GALATIANS 5:22–23

But the fruit of the Spirit is love, joy, peace, forbearance, kindness, goodness, faithfulness, gentleness and self-control. Against such things there is no law.

Orchards are lovely places to walk. A healthy orchard is colorful, vibrant, and, if you listen closely with your imagination rather than with your ears, you will hear the sound of quiet, flourishing *life*. As one of my mentors used to say, "You don't hear grunting in an orchard!" In other words, the trees aren't forcing their fruit to emerge; fruit grows naturally on a healthy fruit tree.

And for that tree to flourish, it needs a particular type of soil, a particular kind of weather, and a particular kind of care. If you are a tree planted deeply in the soil of God's love (Eph. 3:17), then the fruit of the Spirit will naturally burst from your branches. It's the way it works.

Love? Yes, we want to selflessly care for others. Joy? Yes, we want to rejoice in the Lord always. Peace? Yes, we want God's deep shalom settling our spirits, bringing peace to those around us. Forbearance? Yes, we want the ability to be patient, to persevere through long and hard times. Kindness? Yes, we want to handle others with a gracious spirit. Goodness? Yes, we want to treat others with dignity as sacred reflections of the image of God.

Faithfulness? Yes, we want to be full of faith, resisting fear, pride, and sin, trusting in God's emerging future more than the circumstances in front of us. Gentleness? Yes, we want to learn the art of being careful in our demeanor, aware of the best ways to approach and serve others. Self-control? Yes. More of that, please; mastery of our own souls by the power of the Spirit is a daily need.

To gain the fruit we want hanging heavy from our branches, how do we yield the tree of our lives to the Spirit's work, remaining planted in the soil of the Father's love and bearing expressions of character that look, sound, and impact lives—like Jesus?

First, we can tend to our soil. The Father will take care of us, but we have things we can do to make sure we remain "rooted and established in love." Worship, filling my life (my home, my car, my walks), draws me back to my belovedness again and again. Worship enriches our soil.

Second, we can watch the weather. If the climate we're in is dragging us down and affecting our fruit, we have choices we can make. We can stay in the game and be a weather-changer for everyone's sake. Or there may also be times we need to move to a different climate, in whole (a complete transplant) or in part (taking seasons to hang out in a greenhouse every now and again). We have some level of control over the weather in which we are growing.

Third, we can yield to the steady care that comes from the Father, pruning us, cutting off growth that is natural but drawing strength away from the fruit. The Lord of the orchard is about the work of drawing fruit from us; we can trust the processes that lead to that sweet, flourishing, Jesus-fragrant fruit appearing in our life.

Jesus, I receive the Holy Spirit. Let me be present to the soil, the weather, and the processes that bring the best fruit from my life. Come, Holy Spirit, make my character like the character of Jesus. Let me become a sweet and sustaining gift to those around me. I pray in Jesus' name, amen.

THE QUESTIONS

- Which fruit of the Spirit above is the Lord of the orchard tending to in your life right now?

- What goal do you imagine he has for that aspect of your character coming to maturity?

THE SPIRIT QUENCHES OUR DEEPEST THIRST

JOHN 7:37–39

On the last and greatest day of the festival, Jesus stood and said in a loud voice, "Let anyone who is thirsty come to me and drink. Whoever believes in me, as Scripture has said, rivers of living water will flow from within them." By this he meant the Spirit, whom those who believed in him were later to receive. Up to that time the Spirit had not been given, since Jesus had not yet been glorified.

There is an unseen current rushing through your home, your church, and your city. That current is nudging everything it touches, and letting us know it's there. It is the mighty river of the Holy Spirit, and it's coming to . . . no, it's already flowing through . . . a location near you. Whether or not we allow that river to flow in through the gateway of our hearts, to the deepest places, to satisfy our deepest longings, and to then become a spring of living, satisfying water that flows from us to others—is a choice we all have to make.

In John 7, Jesus is attending the Festival of Tabernacles (or *Sukkot*), a feast that commemorates the shelter-living the Jews had to do as they wandered through the wilderness on their way to the Holy Land. It was in that wilderness that water miraculously flowed from a rock to satisfy the desert-thirst of God's people. On the very "last and greatest day" of that celebration of the exodus journey toward the promised land, Jesus lifted up his voice for all to hear: "Let anyone who is thirsty come to me and drink. Whoever believes in me . . . rivers of living water will flow from within them."

First, the stories of the exodus would have leapt to mind for those listening, potentially feeling parched themselves. The Jews needed water. God provided. Second, Jesus seems to be suggesting that thirst will be quenched for a believer by a river of "living water," gushing up from within. This phrasing feels quite similar to Jesus' words, spoken to the Samaritan woman in John 4. Jesus is most probably drawing their attention to verses like Jeremiah 2:13, a powerful prophetic passage: "My people have committed two sins: 'They have forsaken me, the spring of living water, and have dug their own cisterns, broken cisterns that cannot hold water.'"

Broken cisterns. Our best human efforts to satisfy our spiritual thirst ultimately leave us desperate and unsatisfied. Jesus is saying that unquenched thirst is an indicator that someone's cisterns are broken, and our best efforts to replace what God gives are not enough. Jesus also knows that we need to know our need, to really *feel* our lack, before we pursue him for spiritual satisfaction.

Pray to become, and to remain, a thirsty believer—one who relies on, and drinks from, the river of the Spirit flowing from within. The life of Jesus flowing from within. Ask God to help you identify any broken cisterns you have made to satisfy your own spiritual thirst. Then pray for those in your home, church, and city to become aware of their own need as well.

The river of the Spirit is there for the drinking; lead others to the water that you have found.

Jesus, I receive the Holy Spirit. There is a river of life within me, and I welcome both the refreshing I need and the call to meet the thirst needs of others. Come, Holy Spirit, let your Holy Spirit pour from life, sweeping those in my influence up in your current of love. I pray in Jesus' name, amen.

THE QUESTION

- How would you define "spiritual thirst," and how have you experienced Jesus quenching that thirst in you?

A DESERT CAN LEAD TO A DESTINY

LUKE 4:1–2, 14–15

Jesus, full of the Holy Spirit, left the Jordan and was led by the Spirit into the wilderness, where for forty days he was tempted by the devil. He ate nothing during those days, and at the end of them he was hungry. . . . Jesus returned to Galilee in the power of the Spirit, and news about him spread through the whole countryside. He was teaching in their synagogues, and everyone praised him.

A desert can lead to a destiny. A dark night can lead to a bright day. A wilderness can lead to awakening. Who would choose to take a forty-day, fasting-prayer-walk in a barren, wild, dangerous, and lifeless place? Probably none of us. But who needs that kind of journey, at least on a spiritual level, to shake us out of our dull sleep into full spiritual alertness to what the Father is doing? All of us. We all need that kind of ongoing awakening. The Spirit works to awaken us in the *desert*.

When Jesus went into the wilderness, he was "full of the Holy Spirit." When he returned from the wilderness, he returned in the "power of the Spirit." Something happened in that liminal space between death and life—that place where temptations rage to unseat us from our place of intimacy with the Father.

In his desert, the Son of Man resisted until both the temptations and the tempter lost agency (lost power) to extract him from the love of the Father. Lesser loves couldn't move him; in his baptismal waters, the love question had been settled for the King of kings—he knew who he was, whose he was, and why he was. The desert brings it all to the surface, to test if it's real.

There is a painting of Jesus in the desert by the Russian artist Ivan Kramskoi. Created in 1872, it is called, "Christ in the Desert," and it captures the Lord in one of the most human ways I've ever seen in a work of art. His eyes have the haunting look of one both fasting and fighting, all captured in the same image. I've felt that way the past few years—spiritually faithful and spiritually fitful—all in the same moments. Let's apply the story of Jesus in the desert to you and me.

Personal challenges, pandemics, political unrest, polarizing issues, perfect storms in relationships—they can all serve as desert-to-destiny experiences for those of us who walk into them full of the Holy Spirit. We go into deserts like one kind of person, and by the Spirit's power, we can come out another. Without the formation that occurs in the desert, are we ever truly prepared to lead anyone in anything?

With so much isolation, anxiety, and anger streaming over the airwaves in our time, Christians continue to face a daily temptation to serve someone or something other than Jesus. We are challenged, as Jesus was in the wilderness, as to who we will serve, and from whom we will take our cues. This season is an opportune time to evaluate who we will follow into the future, and who will get our primary allegiance—no matter what it requires of us.

In the desert, the Spirit will help us choose Jesus—and the desert will lead us to our destiny, our destination, as a beloved child of God.

Jesus, I receive the Holy Spirit. I want to be filled with your Spirit, again and again, and to emerge from my deserts moving in the power of the Spirit. Come, Holy Spirit, empty me of myself in order to fill me with yourself. I pray in Jesus' name, amen.

THE QUESTION

- What recent desert have you been through, and did you emerge stronger in the power of the Holy Spirit?

THE SPIRIT OF RESURRECTION LIVES IN YOU

ROMANS 8:11

And if the Spirit of him who raised Jesus from the dead is living in you, he who raised Christ from the dead will also give life to your mortal bodies because of his Spirit who lives in you.

I would like to officially announce the launch of a new form of communication for followers of Jesus, called "resurrection-speak." Resurrection-speak is a form of communication in which our words, actions, and calendars reveal to everyone around us that we are a people who are raised with Christ (Rom. 6:4; Col. 3:1), and who plan to live *forever*.

Resurrection-speak is the kind of talk that comes out of a person who is living, as Irenaeus of Lyons put it, "fully alive" in the presence of the Father.

We are raised with Christ *now*, we are filled with the Spirit *now*, we are motivated by a new and living hope *now*. Our baptism imaged it in a way that is more than a symbol. Symbols are simply pictures of ideas. Baptism is a sacred *action*; it is an action that, as Evelyn

Underhill put it, actually *does* something.[6] Like the exchange of a wedding ring or a welcome embrace, when you and I were baptized, it *did* something in us—it performed a work within us—it marked that we were no longer dead in sin; we were raised with Christ.

Resurrection-speak is full of faith, full of hope, and full of love (1 Cor. 13:13). It sounds shockingly assured of things we hope for, confident of things that are unseen by the naked eye (Heb. 11:1). Resurrection-speak comes from a heart that is so aligned with the new creation ahead that it injects its promises into the now without even thinking.

The prayers for others that emerge from someone who practices resurrection-speak have a ring of spiritual authority, and reveal a more-than-a-conqueror faith (Rom. 8:37) behind it. Those prayers don't sound like waffling attempts at poetry, well-intentioned to comfort but based more on the sincere compassion of the pray-er than on the steadfast promises of God (2 Cor. 1:20).

If the "Spirit of him who raised Jesus from the dead" lives in you (Rom. 8:11), then the Spirit gets to do the talking, the acting, and the planning. Would the Father communicate continual worry, despair, anxiety, or fear in the face of challenging situations? Would the Father communicate the sorry story that hope is elusive, God's intervention is sporadic, or sin is an option? Would the Father plan a calendar that doesn't include seasons of prayer, caring for the poor, or gathering to worship with the saints?

Along with you, my mortal body needs some spiritual life right now. Don't wait for eternity to be-up, show-up, or to sing-up the faith that has been strengthening believers to be like Jesus for millennia.

---

6. Evelyn Underhill, *Worship* (Cambridge: James Clarke & Co. 1937, 2010), 43.

Holy Spirit, teach us the art of resurrection-speak—until our lives match up with your promises.

THE PRAYER

Jesus, I receive the Holy Spirit. You have said that I will live forever, in your loving presence. Come, Holy Spirit, help me live my life in light of the eternity that is ahead. I pray in Jesus' name, amen.

THE QUESTIONS

- How do your words, actions, and calendar reveal where your hope lies?

- Is there anything you could change in any one of those categories that resonates more fully with the reality that you are a new creation, a raised-from-the-dead disciple of Jesus?

THE FATHER GIVES THE SPIRIT, AND WE DO OUR PART

LUKE 11:13

"If you then, though you are evil, know how to give good gifts to your children, how much more will your Father in heaven give the Holy Spirit to those who ask him!"

Like many Christians I know, I have had the privilege of praying for many people over the years. In churches, in conferences, at the mechanic's garage, and in restaurants, I've tried to get beyond my natural introversion to obey Jesus to pray for anyone he leads me to. Like some of you, over the years I've prayed for hundreds of people for healing of the heart, mind, and body, for encouragement, for freedom from long-standing sins, for the Holy Spirit to fill them, or for the love of the Father to overwhelm them.

In all those cases, I am glad we prayed, glad we took the step of faith, and glad we discovered the Holy Spirit is always at work in very unique ways. I've often seen people experience God's love powerfully, but I've seen people experience physical healing far less frequently.

When we pray for one another, praying from a place of devotion to Jesus, clear-heartedness, and faith, the Father gives the gift of the Holy Spirit. It's a fact, according to Luke 11:13. We may see something dramatic occur, or something very normal occur. If someone leaves with a deeper sense of the Father's love, I'm over-the-moon happy! But I've still wondered why I don't see more physical healing when I pray.

When I am discouraged, feeling like the Holy Spirit is not being given as lavishly in the moment as I would like, I remember the words of John Wimber, a mentor of mine. He encouraged us to pray for at least a thousand people or more before we started evaluating if our prayers worked or not related to physical healing. I see others praying for physical healing, and God answering those prayers in profound and unique ways. What gives?

I asked this question of another mentor of mine many years ago who traveled around the world and often saw people physically healed. He doesn't hype things up—he's seen some crazy, beautiful things happen in many lives. I asked him, "Why doesn't God heal through me? Is there something I'm doing wrong?" I didn't expect the answer he gave.

"Dan, the Holy Spirit is healing people through his church all over the world. Why does it have to be through you for it to be happening?" He was giving me a heart check. Seeing healing occur was more about me than I thought.

Yes, my compassion wants things to be fixed for people. Like you, when we pray, we often connect deeply with the love of the Father for a person. But he is doing more than I can see in that person's life. There are many paths through which God heals. And his timing is perfect. Do I need to be the center of a physical healing ministry? Or is it possible that God will use me on occasion in that way, and he will use others on occasion in the same way he uses me now?

The Father is pouring out his Holy Spirit on his church. Your work, and mine, is to trust that is true, and to join the Father in the work he is doing right in front of us. We pray for anyone, and everyone, we can. If a spontaneous healing occurs, wonderful. If not, all is well; remind those you pray for to rest in the Father's love in their suffering, and that you'll continue to pray for their healing. Then, we keep praying, and we keep showing up to do our part in faith.

The rest is up to the Father; he is healing, and transforming lives, through his church.

THE PRAYER

Jesus, I receive the Holy Spirit. Where I have become discouraged and doubted that you are doing great things in the world today, change my perspective. Come, Holy Spirit, give me a passion to pray for others and to expect your miracles—no matter what form they may take. I pray in Jesus' name, amen.

THE QUESTIONS

- Can you think of someone for whom you could pray for physical healing this week?

- If so, how could you ask them if they'd be willing for you to pray for them?

THE WAY OF LOVE: THE FOUNDATION FOR SPIRITUAL GIFTS

1 CORINTHIANS 13:1–7

If I speak in the tongues of men or of angels, but do not have love, I am only a resounding gong or a clanging cymbal. If I have the gift of prophecy and can fathom all mysteries and all knowledge, and if I have a faith that can move mountains, but do not have love, I am nothing. If I give all I possess to the poor and give over my body to hardship that I may boast, but do not have love, I gain nothing.

Love is patient, love is kind. It does not envy, it does not boast, it is not proud. It does not dishonor others, it is not self-seeking, it is not easily angered, it keeps no record of wrongs. Love does not delight in evil but rejoices with the truth. It always protects, always trusts, always hopes, always perseveres.

So, here we are: heaven-meets-earth people, the beloved of the Father, filled with and empowered by the indwelling Holy Spirit (Rom. 8:11), seated in heavenly places with Jesus (Eph. 2:6), ready to enter another day as the royal priesthood (1 Peter 2:9), relying on God's love, learning to live in love (1 John 4:16), to move about in time and space as the people of the resurrection. How will the Spirit work through you, through me, today?

Spiritual gifts, especially those noted in 1 Corinthians, have long been a fascination of the body of Christ. These "gracelets" from heaven, expressing ministry in Jesus' name, have been a curiosity for the church ever since Jesus released his disciples to do miracles and the Spirit was poured out at Pentecost. Spiritual gifts should be eagerly desired by anyone wanting to be filled with the Holy Spirit and empowered to do what Jesus did. But we must first learn to do what Jesus did in the *way*, in the *why*, he did what he did (John 14:12–14).

And to this point, Paul wants to make something clear. The progression for gifts of the Spirit to be made manifest in the life of a believer is to be as follows: "Follow the way of love and eagerly desire gifts of the Spirit" (1 Cor. 14:1a). In 1 Corinthians 13, Paul takes an entire chapter to make the way of love very, very clear. If you want the gifts, he is saying, start by learning the way of love. Love is the foundation, the "complete" (love) toward which the incomplete (spiritual gifts) points (1 Cor. 13:8–13).

In other words, love matters *most*. Love is the center, reason, and meaning for any spiritual experience. Love is real where you see it with these characteristics: "Love is patient, love is kind. It does not envy, it does not boast, it is not proud. It does not dishonor others, it is not self-seeking, it is not easily angered, it keeps no record of wrongs. Love does not delight in evil but rejoices with the truth. It always protects, always trusts, always hopes, always perseveres."

We could go so far as to say that, for Paul, love is the most powerful force on earth—and love is the center of all things the Father, Son, and Holy Spirit do in the universe.

There is nowhere to hide from these words of Paul, and we brush them off to our peril. If we're even going to begin to talk about spiritual gifts, the prerequisite is a long, drawn out, life-long course on *love*. The Jesus-kind of love is mingled with everlasting truth—it is not sappy or sentimental, it is in accord with the essential character and reality of God. We have seen enough confusion created by love-immature leaders who gain their identity from hyped spiritual power sessions. The Father wrote Jesus' business card in his baptismal waters—*beloved*. The Christian's heart must first know it is beloved, and be artful at expressing love and compassion, for gifts of spiritual power to be expressed healthily and fruitfully through each one of us.

If the Spirit is training you in love, and you are leaning into love's life curriculum, you are in the right spot for being used in spiritual gifts. It's time to learn to step into spiritual gifts as we remain in love's gravitational pull.

THE PRAYER

Jesus, I receive the Holy Spirit. I want to be used in various forms of spiritual gifts. I know that first means you want to teach me the way of love. Come, Holy Spirit, teach me to love as Jesus did, without reserve and without condition. I pray in Jesus' name, amen.

THE QUESTIONS

- Have you ever experienced a spiritual gift in action that you would put in the category of beyond natural gifting?

- If so, did you sense that the deep love of the Father was involved and expressed in the experience?

DAY 48

WHY IT IS GOOD TO BE INFORMED ABOUT SPIRITUAL GIFTS

1 CORINTHIANS 12:1–2

Now about the gifts of the Spirit, brothers and sisters, I do not want you to be uninformed. You know that when you were pagans, somehow or other you were influenced and led astray to mute idols.

You may know the story of the Japanese intelligence officer who continued to defend his island in the Philippines for twenty-nine years after World War II was officially over. It took a visit from his commanding officer (a fashionably late visit, mind you) to relieve him of his duty. While various attempts at communication had been made, they were met with skepticism because of his internal commitment to his previous orders. He remained *uninformed* about the new world order that had come about. What we don't know can, truly, kill us—or at the very least, it can confuse us, and bring harm to us and through us, for a very long time.

Paul did not want his new family, the community of Christ, to be uninformed about either spiritual gifts or the "new creation order" behind their practice. The new creation order behind the spiritual gifts was that the love of God had been embodied and expressed in

Christ Jesus (John 3:16), and that same love was now poured out on the church by the Spirit (Rom. 5:5), a loved-to-life community (Rom. 8:31–39) who would then follow the way of Jesus in offering themselves in loving service to the world. If we get any part of that wrong, Corinthian Christian or present-day Christian, we get everything wrong that follows.

Gifts are for *loving service.*

In Corinth, it seems they were active in practicing various forms of spiritual gifts. But when the why behind a practice is off, everything is off. The motivation determines the manifestation. The converted pagan Corinthians had previous orders still at work in their bones related to handling spiritual power. Corinth was literally a magical place, a center for playing with spiritual powers and for receiving instruction on how to get them to do your will. They had a few things to unlearn. Christianity is as much about unlearning what we've known as it is about learning what we previously did not know.

When they became Christians they may have had, by intuition, a perception of how and why spiritual power works. Was that intuition right? No, it was wrong. The way they practiced spiritual gifts, and the fruit that blossomed from those practices, didn't represent the heart of Jesus. Now, they were learning to respond to the Holy Spirit's presence and leadership. Learning to follow the Spirit takes as much unlearning as it takes learning, as much emptying as filling.

By addressing their pagan background, Paul is dividing their past pagan paradigm from their new Paracletic paradigm. Magic is what we do to manipulate a spiritual force to do our will. The Corinthians had their spiritual dispositions formed in a pagan approach to manipulating and controlling deities. Paul wanted to be clear with the Corinthians that life in the Spirit is the utter opposite of manipulative magic—it is the path of obedient self-offering.

Today, unbiblical and distorted cultural views of love, power, and personal achievement have a great and sometimes hidden influence on how we approach spiritual gifts. Our work is to become aware of our belovedness, be healed by that belovedness, and to then become lovers of God and people in the overflow.

We will then have the capacity to be selfless in our approach to the things of the Spirit, partnering in what the Father is already doing, as Jesus did (John 5:19). Intimacy with God enables us to perceive—spiritual ears and eyes open—what God is doing in someone's life right in front of us.

The gifts are then used in accord with their purpose; they are expressions of loving grace poured out from the Father. Our work is to allow the Spirit to use us as flow-through vessels for the winning of hearts and the healing of souls.

THE PRAYER

Jesus, I receive the Holy Spirit. I am eager to learn the way of love so I can perceive what you are already doing in another's life, and join you in that work. Come, Holy Spirit, reveal to me where my culture is informing my motivations more than my intimacy with you. I pray in Jesus' name, amen.

THE QUESTION

- Consider your own perspectives on love, power, and self-achievement. How might those perspectives be more shaped by your years of experience rather than by the Scriptures and the Spirit?

YOUR SPIRITUAL GIFT IS BETTER THAN MY SPIRITUAL GIFT?

1 CORINTHIANS 12:4–6

There are different kinds of gifts, but the same Spirit distributes them. There are different kinds of service, but the same Lord. There are different kinds of working, but in all of them and in everyone it is the same God at work.

Have you ever seen someone else's gifts in action and thought, *My goodness, it's not fair that God gifted them like that! I can only do (fill in the blank)*. It's like we're in junior high all over again, ranking ourselves compared to others based on measures like "smart," "athletic," "pretty," or "popular." Or, perhaps you were on the other end of the relational spectrum in junior high, noting your own gifts, and determining that your giftedness somehow made you more special than others.

That is where the Corinthians found themselves, and we, left to our own thinking, feelings, judgments, and celebrity-cultural reflexes, can find ourselves there as well. In the former case, the sins driving our self-abasement are *fear* and *unbelief*. In the latter case, the sins driving our self-aggrandizement are *pride* and *arrogance*. In both cases, sin makes us think different gifts determine our different levels of value, and value to God. Our measures are skewed, and those measures have a terrible impact on what we do and don't do as followers of Jesus.

In this passage, Paul is talking to the Corinthians about what happens when they worship, when they have come together as the community of the Spirit to be nourished at Christ's table. So he levels the playing field. The gifts, Paul explains, while having different applications and effects, are all spiritual manifestations and gifts of grace from the Spirit of God. The Spirit owns and hands out the gifts; no one has them as if they are special and others are not.

He is making clear that all believers have gifts distributed by the Holy Spirit, while not all are used in the same gifts at all times. Then (as now) flashier or more unusual gifts got special attention. People thought they were better than one another, or worse than one another—and the way they responded in relationships quietly perpetuated the unholy cycle. There is truly nothing new under the sun. When our cultural values get in the driver's seat of our hearts, there is always a spiritual accident waiting to happen.

Let's put it bluntly so we get it. The Holy Spirit is at work in the world, through the church. The Holy Spirit fills and empowers the community of Christ, and individual believers within it, to live with the character of Jesus in the world (Gal. 5:22–23), and to do what Jesus did (John 14:12–14). The Holy Spirit fills the people of God, followers of Jesus, as a temple of living stones, being built together (1 Peter 2:5), who then demonstrate the kingdom of God is among us before the people in our homes, churches, and cities. The Spirit is the eschatological Spirit[7] who brings the new creation life of the future into the now, and performs wonders through God's people that signal that bright future ahead. You and I have the Holy Spirit

---

7. Gordon Fee, *Paul, the Spirit, and the People of God* (Grand Rapids: Baker Academic, 1996), ix.

DAN WILT

in us, and with us. The Spirit distributes gifts of grace to us, and through us, that provide for our shared spiritual nourishment in worship, that strengthen the church as a body, and that further the reach of the gospel to the ends of the earth.

If you think someone is better than you because of the way God uses them, you have a heart problem that needs emergency surgery. They are called to bear the same fruits of the Spirit that you are, the very character of Christ. Yes, learn from them, be inspired by their obedience—but don't unduly elevate them as you simultaneously diminish the gifts of God at work in you.

If you think someone is less important than you because of the way God uses you, you also have a heart problem that needs emergency surgery. Be grateful for the ways God uses you, but learn from the humility of others what spiritual giftedness looks like when it's off a stage and doesn't need a microphone to give it volume.

THE PRAYER

Jesus, I receive the Holy Spirit. Work in my heart as I learn to embrace the gifts of the Spirit in all their forms, as gifts of grace from you. Come, Holy Spirit, help me to use the gifts you have invested in me, and to be used by you in gifts that come in a moment of need, for your glory. I pray in Jesus' name, amen.

THE QUESTIONS

- Have you ever taken a spiritual gift test?

- If so, in what ways have you found that God consistently uses you to show others the heart of Jesus?

THE GREAT SYMPHONY OF SPIRITUAL GIFTS

1 CORINTHIANS 12:7

Now to each one the manifestation of the Spirit
is given for the common good.

Every once in a while, I do something to up my cultural game. I attend a symphony. And one of my favorite moments at the symphony is when the music is not playing at all.

The moment of which I am speaking occurs soon after the chaotic sound of the orchestral instruments, simultaneously being tuned up, has died down. While I am fond of the tuning session because I enjoy the creative process, I wouldn't want to listen to two hours of everyone fiddling around with their instruments. Though each musician brings decades of natural gifting, passion, training, and cultivated, inspiring talent to the moment, the tuning portion of the night has them all playing out of accord, doing their own thing, creating a cacophonous wall of disordered sound with no dynamic variation and little attention to what the others are doing.

My favorite moment is the pregnant pause located between the tuning portion of the night and the start of the concert. That moment is electric with anticipation. These virtuoso performers are about to submit their years of experience and their best individual gifts to a shared piece of music.

Yes, there will be solos, duets, quartets, and instances in which the whole orchestra will sound their voices at the same time. But the greatest, hidden joy we will all experience is that the musicians are playing, all together, for a common purpose. They will play for that common purpose, and they will be silent for that common purpose. Some may leave the stage for that common purpose, and others will sound loud and strong for that common purpose.

What is that common purpose, that vocation, that calling? To play the music before them. The musical score is the star of the night; not the individual musicians. Their instrumental diversity will be submitted to their vocational unity, and their vocational unity will be remarkable because of their instrumental diversity. Joy, and beauty, will be the result. For you and for me, Jesus is the music, and we each have a part to play.

"To each one the manifestation of the Spirit is given for the common good."

"To each one . . ." Paul means each person. He means you. He means me. In this context, he means every person who is following Jesus and is a part of the communion of the *ekklesia*, the called-out ones, the church. In other words, each one of us has an instrument in our hands. Practice and mentoring have brought us to this opportunity to play—*together*.

"The manifestation of the Spirit is given . . ." Paul uses a variety of terms to talk about spiritual expression and gifts in 1 Corinthians 12. He used a term that means "things of the Spirit" in verse 1. He used a term that means "gifts of grace from the Spirit" in verse 4. Here in verse 7 he uses the phrase "manifestation of the Spirit" to express something like a display or an exhibition of the Spirit's presence and goodness. In other words, we each have music we were uniquely made to make, to put God's glory on display.

But now, our reason for receiving the unique "manifestation of the Spirit" that is ours is made crystal clear.

"For the common good." The phrase for "common good" speaks of a symphony—coming together for a purpose, a shared vocation, a calling as a family. In a family symphony, your good is why I am gifted. My good is why you are gifted. Our common good as the body of Christ is why we have been given these gifts of grace—to build up the church in our most holy faith and to keep us in God's love (Jude 1:20–21). The overflow of the symphonic unity of the church in the sharing of spiritual gifts will result in the common good of our homes, churches, and cities. Awakening in the world lies on the other side of the awakening of the church.

The Father has written our music, the Son is our melody, and the Spirit is teaching us to play it together—for the sake of the world Jesus loves.

THE PRAYER

Jesus, I receive the Holy Spirit. I honor you today by recognizing that I have been given a unique manifestation of the Spirit for the common good. Come, Holy Spirit, teach me how to serve others well in my community as I champion the common good of your church. I pray in Jesus' name, amen.

THE QUESTION

- What is it that you do that, when you do it, you feel the life of the Spirit at work in you—and others seem to respond in a way that they are drawn closer to God?

THE GIFTS OF THE SPIRIT ARE MANY AND ABUNDANT

1 CORINTHIANS 12:8–11

To one there is given through the Spirit a message of wisdom, to another
a message of knowledge by means of the same Spirit, to another faith by
the same Spirit, to another gifts of healing by that one Spirit, to another
miraculous powers, to another prophecy, to another distinguishing between
spirits, to another speaking in different kinds of tongues, and to still another
the interpretation of tongues. All these are the work of one and the same
Spirit, and he distributes them to each one, just as he determines.

I like a good list, don't you? In fact, I keep mine as mementos of things I haven't completed. While my wife dutifully creates a list on any given day, and checks off each item with delight, my lists tend have more of an *optional* feel to them; each list is an ever-changing piece of scribbled art scattered among others on my desk, documenting my best intentions and a few of my shining accomplishments. I don't know what I'd do without my lists; I've grown quite attached to them.

For whatever reasons we make them, we are creatures of lists. But when it comes to spiritual gifts, our tendency to make lists out of the wide range of manifestations of the Spirit and gifts of grace in the Bible may get in the way of us understanding the point. In 1 Corinthians 12:8–11 there are nine spiritual gifts listed (*charismata*, or "gracelets").

Is that it? Do we have our list?

Unfortunately, it's not that simple, which is why we have so many different counts and perspectives on spiritual gifts today. In Romans 12:6–8, more gifts are added to our list, gifts like serving, teaching, encouraging, giving, and leading. That list feels like it's starting to lean toward what we might call "natural gifts" in people to which the Spirit gives divine impetus at key moments. Then, in Ephesians 4:11 we note that there are gifts which some people seem to express with regularity, i.e., apostles, prophets, evangelists, pastors, and teachers. In still other places, gifts like hospitality (1 Peter 4:9–10), celibacy (1 Cor. 7:7–8), and martyrdom (1 Cor. 13:3) can be understood to be gifts of grace from the Holy Spirit.

In fact, going one step farther, have you ever met a non-Christian who had a profound gift you knew was something God had given them, like creativity or friendship, that seemed to be made for a higher purpose than that for which they were using it? I have, many times. Attributing someone's profound gift of creativity or the ability to cultivate friendship to anyone other than God, regardless of how they are using that gift, feels like an ill-fit. The person bears the image of God; why wouldn't they evidence something of his nature, distorted and broken as that expression might be?

Given all we have learned about the Holy Spirit so far, and the wide diversity of God's displays of creativity in people and creation, we can conclude that there may be different categories of spiritual gifts that all come from the same source. Some gifts are prospered natural gifts (like a teaching or leadership gift), and some are given as God chooses (like healing, miracles, or a prayer language/

tongues) when we come to faith and mature in Christ. All gifts from the Spirit are for our edification, and for "the common good" (1 Cor. 12:7).

Paul's goal, it seems, was not to give us a textbook on spiritual gifts. If it was, he would have gone into far more detail as a Spirit-filled, Spirit-led teacher. It seems the Holy Spirit's goal was to give us a framework for understanding *that* God's grace works within us, *how* God's grace works within us, and *why* God's grace works within us. From service, to miracles, to speaking by the power of the Spirit,[8] God is awakening his church to serve the world.

THE PRAYER

Jesus, I receive the Holy Spirit. I open myself to the outpouring of your Spirit in my life. Come, Holy Spirit, as I serve others, expand my natural gifts with your divine power, and teach me how to be open to be used in special gifts that you give for a moment of encounter with your love. I pray in Jesus' name, amen.

THE QUESTION

- In the list of gifts mentioned in 1 Corinthians 12:8–11, which ones would you most like to learn more about? Why?

---

8. Gordon Fee, *Paul, the Spirit, and the People of God* (Grand Rapids: Baker Academic, 1996), 165.

THE SPIRITUAL GIFTS BUILD LOCAL CHURCHES

ROMANS 12:4–8

For just as each of us has one body with many members, and these
members do not all have the same function, so in Christ we, though
many, form one body, and each member belongs to all the others. We
have different gifts, according to the grace given to each of us. If your
gift is prophesying, then prophesy in accordance with your faith; if it
is serving, then serve; if it is teaching, then teach; if it is to encourage,
then give encouragement; if it is giving, then give generously; if it
is to lead, do it diligently; if it is to show mercy, do it cheerfully.

I'll be honest. There have been times I have been around very spiritually gifted people, and I felt like we mutually "belonged" to one
another. They approached their gift with humility and compassion,
and I felt the Spirit of Jesus in their demeanor. They ministered to
me with their gifts, and to our church community, and to this day I
am a stronger Christ-follower because of their generosity of spirit.

There have been other times when I've been around very spiritually gifted people, even those who many in the room held in high
esteem because of their unique or remarkable gifts, and yet I felt
that I didn't "belong" to them—nor they to me. Their expression
of a spiritual gift, maybe in the way they presented it, gave me
the sense that they were there as much for themselves as for me.

I don't judge them; I could have been wrong in my discernment—but it's the way it felt.

We are, as Paul puts it, members who "belong" to all the others. That's why spiritual gifts are best applied in a local church where people know our name and it's harder to hide our motivations. Time and familiarity have a way of exposing both our strengths and our weaknesses. If gifts of grace are given for service, starting at home is Christianity 101.

How can we contribute to one another's maturation process on a local level? First of all, let's put stages and platforms aside. They often just confuse things, like who our audience is and why we are offering our gifts. Jesus was never impressed with stages (John 7), and certainly had little good to say to those who were interested in putting on a spiritual show (Matt. 23:5a).

The gift of *prophecy* means that we have cultivated a listening ear to the Holy Spirit, and receive clear guidance that we humbly share with others for their strengthening, encouragement, and comfort (1 Cor. 14:3). The gift of *serving* means that we are someone who eagerly helps others at their point of need, gladly, and without needing continual affirmation or accolades for our work. The gift of *teaching* means that we have deeply studied the Scriptures and the spiritual challenges of our generation, and we can help others apply the gospel in their daily life.

The gift of *encouragement* means that we have a knack for using our words and actions to lift others toward hope when they need a boost. The gift of *giving* means that we have the ability to generate resources, and to then offer them extravagantly and sacrificially to others without a need for recognition or payback. The gift of *leadership* means that we are able to serve, inspire, and guide others on a path that leads to the shared goals we all desire to achieve. The gift of *mercy* means that we express Christ's compassion to those in need of ministry or provision.

A local body, functioning with these and other gifts, given freely to one another by its members, will thrive together. We will become a community of the Spirit, those who belong to one another (Eph. 4:25), encourage one another (1 Thess. 5:11), and are devoted to one another in honoring love (Rom. 12:10).

THE PRAYER

Jesus, I receive the Holy Spirit. I recognize that you have given me spiritual gifts to apply as a servant in my community. Come, Holy Spirit, teach me through others how to use those gifts wisely and in the way of Christ, and empower me to build up our local body. I pray in Jesus' name, amen.

THE QUESTIONS

- Can you describe a circumstance in which someone ministered to you from a place of selflessness and compassion?

- How did it build you up, and/or others around you?

THE BODY IS STRENGTHENED THROUGH SPIRIT-GIFTED LEADERS

EPHESIANS 4:11–13

So Christ himself gave the apostles, the prophets, the evangelists, the pastors and teachers, to equip his people for works of service, so that the body of Christ may be built up until we all reach unity in the faith and in the knowledge of the Son of God and become mature, attaining to the whole measure of the fullness of Christ.

Over the last few years, I have become very aware of my body. I became aware of my need for more cardiovascular exercise when I discovered a heart condition, so I went to the gym where I could be inspired by (and learn from) the athletic types. I became aware of my need for surgery when I tore most of the muscles in my left shoulder in a biking accident—so I looked for a surgeon. I became aware of my need to learn more about how my body works during a challenging health crisis, so I looked for teachers who could explain things to me.

When the body aches, the heart searches for body builders—those who can help us get strong in places where we are weak. That's the way it is with the body of Christ. The Holy Spirit loves the body of Christ. The Holy Spirit knows the body of Christ. And the Holy Spirit is leading the body of Christ to health. How is the Spirit doing this? Through giving spiritual gifts to individuals that build—that strengthen—the body. When the body aches, the heart searches—and the Spirit meets us with those gifted to help us in key areas of need.

I have a friend who loves to plant churches, to care for them and their leaders, and seems to have spiritual authority sometimes marked by powerful ministry expressions. That's someone with an apostolic gifting. I have another friend who hears from the Lord with remarkable clarity, and offers what they hear with humility and for the strengthening and comfort of their local church. That's someone with a prophetic gifting. I have a friend who naturally leads people to put their faith in Jesus. That's someone with an evangelistic gifting. I have another friend who cares for groups of people with wisdom, counsel, and a shepherd's hand. That's someone with a pastoral gifting. I have yet another friend who reads the Scriptures with revelatory insight and communicates their meaning with refreshing clarity. That's someone with a teaching gift.

The body needs all these kinds of leaders to grow. While I don't think any one of the leaders and influencers needs to create a business card with one's title on it (Can you imagine John with a business card that said "Apostle" beneath his name?), I do believe these gifts are real and help the church to flourish.

But the end game of these gifts is not to provide a stage or platform for the gifted; the end game of these gifts is to train us to do what they do, and to help us all become mature in our walk with Jesus. When we don't equip others with and through our gifts, we utterly miss the reason for which we have been gifted in the first place. These gifts call us to Christ, into Christ, and onward with Christ as we deepen in his character.

The whole measure of the fullness of Christ. That's what I want. That's what you want, I trust. We'll need community members who are humble, Scripture-soaked, and fruit-of-the-Spirit leaders with apostolic, prophetic, evangelistic, pastoral, and teaching gifts to help us get there.

THE PRAYER

Jesus, I receive the Holy Spirit. I thank you that you never leave your body without what we need to come to maturity in Christ. Come, Holy Spirit, send your body, in my local church and in the wider church you love, leaders with the kinds of gifts and the character we need to grow. I pray in Jesus' name, amen.

THE QUESTIONS

- Have you recently been ministered to deeply by someone with the kinds of spiritual gifts mentioned in this passage?

- What was your experience?

THE HOLY SPIRIT SPEAKS TO US THROUGH THE SCRIPTURES

2 TIMOTHY 3:14–17

But as for you, continue in what you have learned and have become
convinced of, because you know those from whom you learned it,
and how from infancy you have known the Holy Scriptures, which
are able to make you wise for salvation through faith in Christ Jesus.
All Scripture is God-breathed and is useful for teaching, rebuking,
correcting and training in righteousness, so that the servant of
God may be thoroughly equipped for every good work.

When it comes to the spiritual gifts, in all their forms, learning
how to follow the Spirit's leading, or voice, is vital. Whether we're
talking about management gifts or miracle gifts, every follower of
Jesus needs to learn how to discern the Holy Spirit's leading in real
times, in real places. Perceiving the Spirit's guidance enables us to
express the way of love (1 Cor. 14:1) as Jesus did—seeing what the
Father is doing and partnering with him in his work (John 5:19).
That is Kingdom Followership 101.

How do we *hear* the voice of the Spirit speaking, and *see* what the
Father is doing?

Let's own first that we are seated with Christ in heavenly places (Eph. 2:6), filled with the Holy Spirit (Eph. 5:18), guided into truth by the Spirit (John 16:13), led by the Spirit (Rom. 8:14), and are encouraged to keep in step with the Spirit (Gal. 5:25). It seems we are well-equipped to respond to the Spirit's voice with sensitivity and wisdom.

I've found it helpful to ask two vital questions before talking about hearing the Holy Spirit. First, do I have a longing, a deep desire, to hear God's voice for the things that are in his heart for others as well as for me? Second, is that desire to hear God speak for the sake of his glory, the strengthening of his church, and the blessing of others—even if I am not the one who benefits in any way? Even if I am utterly hidden in the process? Getting honest matters if we are going to hear the voice of a God who calls us to "cruciformity," self-giving, in our service to others.

While there are many ways to talk about hearing the voice of God (and obeying), in the next few days we'll look at a few ways of hearing the Spirit—ways of apprehending the Spirit's guidance, that can help us listen well over a lifetime.

First, we hear the Holy Spirit speak through the Scriptures (2 Tim. 3:14–17). The Scriptures are "God-breathed," and the Spirit is God's breath. While Paul was speaking to Timothy about the Hebrew Bible most assuredly, we can apply God's speaking power to the whole of the canon of Scripture. He was telling Timothy that the Scriptures are a reliable source for entire-life guidance.

The whole counsel of the Bible—when we get it deep in our bones, when it has become a source of strength to us, when it is consistently drawn on for wisdom and guidance, and when it is applied in action day after month after year—will help to keep us on the path to life (Ps. 16:11) and in the narrow way of following Jesus.

If we forsake the Scriptures in our spiritual growth, forgetting our need to rely on them, then we lose a large portion of our spiritual hearing. If we will get the Word of God into us, however, the Spirit will access it at all the right moments we need it.

It's like having an internal compass within us. If I sense I am receiving some inner guidance from the Spirit that goes against some aspect of Jesus' teaching, the fruits of the Spirit, the whole counsel of the Scriptures, the unity of the church, etc., then the Scriptures I have hidden in my heart will tug me toward true north so I don't go wrong. The Word of God, hidden in our hearts (Ps. 119:11), can help to keep us on the path that leads to life.

If we remain immersed in the Scriptures, evidencing the fruit of the Spirit and the character of Christ through applying and living that Holy Word, we can gradually learn to trust our impressions and perceptions through practice, knowing our inner compass will keep us aligned with the way of Jesus delivered to us by the Scriptures.

THE PRAYER

Jesus, I receive the Holy Spirit. I want to learn to hear your voice for the sake of encouraging others, your church, and bringing you glory. Come, Holy Spirit, help me to love your Word, to discern your guidance in my spirit through your Word, and cause me to hunger and thirst for its counsel. I pray in Jesus' name, amen.

THE QUESTIONS

- What kinds of direction have you received from the Scriptures in the past that came to you in just the right moment?

- How did it impact your love for, and trust in, the Spirit speaking through the Scriptures?

THE HOLY SPIRIT SPEAKS TO US THROUGH IMPRESSIONS AND INTUITIONS

ACTS 20:22–24

"And now, compelled by the Spirit, I am going to Jerusalem, not knowing what will happen to me there. I only know that in every city the Holy Spirit warns me that prison and hardships are facing me. However, I consider my life worth nothing to me; my only aim is to finish the race and complete the task the Lord Jesus has given me—the task of testifying to the good news of God's grace."

When it comes to hearing and obeying God's voice, we have to move, to some large degree, in the world of the subjective. It would be wonderful if we received an angel-gram every time we made a decision or sensed we were to do something by a voice from heaven saying, "That's it! You're doing the exact right thing!" But that doesn't seem to happen that often for most of us.

The Holy Spirit speaks to us, with more regularity, in the language of impressions and intuitions. And it seems that the Holy Spirit is comfortable with human beings being human beings—with all of our strengths, weaknesses, subjectivity, personal histories, hang-ups, personalities, emotional wiring, maturities, immaturities, and sensitivities coming to the moment of hearing his voice.

Yet while we trust Jesus and Jesus trusts us, we often are not able to trust ourselves—or our impressions or intuitions—because we've headed down the wrong path following those subjective inner leadings at other times in our lives.

When we choose to follow Jesus, the Holy Spirit fills us, and we go into intensive and long-form discipleship training to become spiritual athletes living out the way of Jesus (1 Cor. 9:25–26), to learn the way of love, and to express the fruits of the Spirit. It is in that process that the Father helps us recover wholeness in our senses as he begins to heal and transform us on our journey. He does this for our good and so that he can use our intuitions, thoughts, and feelings to guide us to do his will.

Taking Paul in Acts 20:22–24 as our example, as Scripture-soaked people who are also seeking to live like Jesus in the world, we can learn to receive guidance and to practice obedience in the form of responding to subtle impressions, mental pictures, senses that something is the right thing to do. As we practice obedience, our discernment gets stronger.

Recently I was with my daughter at a restaurant. In public settings, I try to remain open to the Holy Spirit because there may be a life God wants to change. I've seen too many lives transformed by the gospel—why would I want others to continue to live in broken-ness, negatively impacting others and generations beyond them, just because I'm an introvert and don't want to be embarrassed? Jesus is about transformation, so *I* am about transformation. Jesus is about transformation, so *you* are about transformation. As a family, it's our way.

When our waitress walked up to us, two things happened. I had a picture flash in my mind of this young woman in a graduation gown and cap. It came and it went. Then, I had a sense of compassion for her that felt more like Jesus' compassion within me rather than just my own empathy at work. I perceived her life to be difficult, and that she didn't see herself very highly because of repeated failures. This felt like Jesus was in the lead.

When she came over, I took a risk: "Thanks for being such a great waitress. Can I ask you a question?"

"Sure!" she said.

"Are you in school, or are you planning to go back to school?"

"Yes!" she said enthusiastically. Then her voice dropped lower: "But I'm not sure if I should."

There was the clarity I needed, so I went for it. "I really believe that you're to go back to school, and it's going to go well for you. Follow that dream; you're so worth it. There are good things ahead." I didn't mention Jesus because I didn't feel like I needed to this time, but someone else has or will along her path. Her face beamed, and her countenance was brighter the rest of our time there.

Take a chance encouraging people as the Spirit leads you. It's a great, low-risk way to practice following impressions that the Spirit gives. Just be normal, or "naturally supernatural" as my mentors would say, and follow that inner lead. You'll be glad you did.

THE PRAYER

Jesus, I receive the Holy Spirit. I am thankful that your salvation has reached into my thoughts and emotions and is healing them as we walk together. Come, Holy Spirit, give

me impressions and guidance so I can partner with you in
the healing of hearts. I pray in Jesus' name, amen.

THE QUESTIONS

- What kinds of impressions or intuitions have you experienced in your life that you felt were from the Holy Spirit?

- How did you know, and were others positively impacted?

THE HOLY SPIRIT SPEAKS TO US THROUGH THE GIFT OF WISDOM (PART 1)

JAMES 3:13, 17

Who is wise and understanding among you? Let them show it by their good life, by deeds done in the humility that comes from wisdom. . . .

But the wisdom that comes from heaven is first of all pure; then peace-loving, considerate, submissive, full of mercy and good fruit, impartial and sincere.

Wisdom. You won't find the word in the moniker of a new superhero in the Marvel universe, nor will you find it listed in the social media bio of anyone who actually has it or lives by it. Wisdom is a gift of the Spirit (1 Cor. 12:8a), and is a way the Spirit guides the believer. Who wants wisdom and understanding for life today? I do!

Wisdom has definitely not received the kind of Spirit-speaking press that the more remarkable, unusual, or spontaneous spiritual gifts have received. Why? My guess is because wisdom is the polar opposite of a shiny object.

Wisdom is substantial and shows the signs of age. Wisdom moves slowly, humbly, and deliberately, at a pace that can be uncomfortable to our modern sensibilities. Wisdom usually won't fight for its voice to be heard, though it does cry out on the streets (Prov. 1:20). Wisdom is marked often by study and observation, meaning it is usually hard-won over long periods of time. We should always be listening for wisdom and searching for wisdom as if for a treasure (Prov. 2:1–6).

How does the Holy Spirit speak to us through wisdom? The Cambridge online dictionary defines wisdom as "the ability to use your knowledge and experience to make good decisions and judgments."[9] For the Christian, knowledge and experience have an important role to play in being guided by the Holy Spirit, particularly when drawn on in deep accord with the whole counsel of the Scriptures, guided by our impressions, and discerned with the body of Christ.

The Spirit speaks to us through our *knowledge*, helping us to do smart, right, and reasonable things in the power of the Holy Spirit. Education is good. Skills are good. These can contribute to spiritual wisdom (note: they can also get in the way). Neither you nor I need a spontaneous word from God to take care of our bodies, to practically love our neighbor, to teach a class of little ones to read, or to distribute resources to the needy in our town. We have knowledge about these things, and our spiritual wisdom can be enhanced because of that knowledge. The Spirit works through good old common sense, skill, and learning—and these have a part to play in discerning the voice of the Spirit (Rom. 12:2).

Regarding *experience*, our own and others' experiences can help us learn if what we're doing has worked in the past for ourselves and others. While experience must always be submitted to the Scriptures and other means of hearing the Holy Spirit (so we don't assume that God is not doing anything new that might contradict

9. See https://dictionary.cambridge.org/us/dictionary/english/wisdom.

our previous experience), experience can serve us as a key contributor when guidance is needed.

If we keep all of these ways of hearing the Spirit speak before us, allowing them to play their part and have a dynamic interplay, our ability to discern the will of God together will grow.

THE PRAYER

Jesus, I receive the Holy Spirit. There is a way of wisdom that I am eager to walk in as I learn the way of love. Come, Holy Spirit, give me the desire and perseverance I need to be filled with wisdom, and guided by wisdom, as I live out my faith in my home, church, and city. I pray in Jesus' name, amen.

THE QUESTION

- Has there been a situation in your life where a gift of wisdom, coming through you or another person, provided guidance that you can now look back on with thankfulness?

THE HOLY SPIRIT SPEAKS TO US THROUGH THE GIFT OF WISDOM (PART 2)

COLOSSIANS 1:9–12

For this reason, since the day we heard about you, we have not stopped praying for you. We continually ask God to fill you with the knowledge of his will through all the wisdom and understanding that the Spirit gives, so that you may live a life worthy of the Lord and please him in every way: bearing fruit in every good work, growing in the knowledge of God, being strengthened with all power according to his glorious might so that you may have great endurance and patience, and giving joyful thanks to the Father, who has qualified you to share in the inheritance of his holy people in the kingdom of light.

Why is wisdom more useful than knowledge? Because knowing that you don't know everything always works out better than thinking that you do. There is a humility that comes with wisdom, a grounding and awareness of our dependence on God, that the Spirit blesses and prospers. We get the word *humility* from the Latin word for "ground" (*humus*) and we say that a person with wisdom is "down to earth."

Being grounded, humble, and down to earth is the way of Jesus—and is a transformative work the Holy Spirit is about in your life and mine.

In a day when the world's wisdom (or lack thereof), the world's understanding (or lack thereof), and the world's chaos is swirling all about us—demanding our allegiance and confusing our decisions—the Spirit steps in, just as the Spirit did in the beginning (Gen. 1). The Spirit brings God's order, God's perspective, God's meaning in it all to our souls.

Paul's prayer for the Colossians is a powerful prayer we can pray for ourselves and others in the times we are in, that we might be "filled with the knowledge of his will through all the wisdom and understanding that the Spirit gives." If we are filled with "all the wisdom," we'll please him for all the right reasons, bear good fruit, grow in the knowledge of God, and be strengthened with power—resulting in endurance, patience, and thankfulness.

Now that is an inheritance! The kingdom of light is our home!

To be filled with the Father's perspectives is to be aware of what we don't know in this life, and to also be confident in what we do know by faith in the Son of God. It is to be filled with God's understanding as to why that person burst out in hurt and anger, why the systems of the world are built for injustice, and why your team losing the big game is a reasonable outcome—even if thousands of fans were praying for them.

Wisdom will guide our actions, managing how and why we post on social media, what benefit there would be to checking in our neighbor on the anniversary of her husband's passing, and why investing in that young person would be far better than putting a portion of our resources into another stock fund.

If we want to receive all the Holy Spirit has to give, we should learn to love the words of Proverbs 2:1–6:

My son [or daughter], if you accept my words and store up my commands within you, turning your ear to wisdom, and applying your heart to understanding—indeed, if you call out for insight and cry aloud for understanding, and if you look for it as for silver and search for it as for hidden treasure, then you will understand the fear of the LORD and find the knowledge of God. For the LORD gives wisdom; from his mouth come knowledge and understanding.

Holy Spirit, we seek your wisdom and understanding. Fill us with it as we pray.

THE PRAYER

Jesus, I receive the Holy Spirit. I choose the humility that comes with learning at your feet, Lord Jesus. Come, Lord, fill me with the knowledge of your will through all the wisdom and understanding that the Spirit gives. I pray in Jesus' name, amen.

THE QUESTION

- How might it impact your life if you printed off Colossians 1:9–12 and began to pray it every day, for yourself and others, for one week?

THE HOLY SPIRIT SPEAKS TO US THROUGH THE BODY OF CHRIST

ACTS 13:2–3

While they were worshiping the Lord and fasting, the Holy Spirit said, "Set apart for me Barnabas and Saul for the work to which I have called them." So after they had fasted and prayed, they placed their hands on them and sent them off.

ROMANS 12:5

So in Christ we, though many, form one body, and each member belongs to all the others.

In the first centuries of the church, the pagan world of the time was set squarely against the church flourishing. Persecutions played off of, and preyed on, the peculiarity of the body of Christ. Christians didn't think like others in the pagan world of their time (*Your God was crucified?*). Christians didn't value what they valued (*You provide funerals for the poor?*). Christians didn't operate like they operated (*You have a community who practices spiritual gifts and celebrates love, joy, peace—and what?*).

The church was marching to the beat of a different drummer, the Holy Spirit, and the wind of God's presence was at the backs of the believers as they carried Jesus' way of being human into the most unlikely (and dangerous) of worlds. When someone decided they wanted to become a believer, unpopular as it was, they brought all their cultural baggage with them. A long process of catechesis, transformation, and slow integration into the family of Jesus took place—a process in which the new believer learned how to love, how to pray, how to trust, how to exhibit patience, how to handle other human beings, how to worship, and, yes, *how to hear the voice of the Holy Spirit.*

And how did they learn to hear? They learned through mentoring relationships with those who were filled with the Spirit and were walking together by faith—and through the example of the community hearing the Holy Spirit *together.*

As members of one another (Rom. 12:5), spiritually bonded through deep devotion to one another's well-being and formation into Christ, they could trust that the Holy Spirit speaking was for the good of them all. Individualism was far less a problem in the early church than it seems to be today. When you face persecution together, unity in your spiritual family becomes very, very important to you.

And when we see moments like Acts 13:2–3 occur, when the local body of believers was worshiping and fasting, the Holy Spirit would *speak.* We don't know all the details, but we have a sense that the shared mission of the church was owned by all the members. When Barnabas and Saul were launched into ministry, the whole body had heard the Spirit guide them, and the whole body was behind them being sent out to do the work to which the Holy Spirit had called them.

The Spirit speaks through local bodies in which we learn the ways of love, worship, service, giving, growing, being discipled, being encouraged, being challenged, responding with grace, and so on.

It is with a family of believers that we are intended to be trained to hear the Spirit's voice, and to discern the Holy Spirit's guidance about our next steps of faith personally, and about our next steps of faith corporately.

Imperfect as a local community of faith can be, each is intended to be a source of Spirit-guided discernment and insight for our ongoing journey with Jesus.

THE PRAYER

Jesus, I receive the Holy Spirit. I thank you for the body of Christ, and for how I am being formed by the friendships and encouragements that come as we walk together. Come, Holy Spirit, speak to me through the body of Christ, and teach me the way of love so I can participate well in that shared hearing for the road ahead. I pray in Jesus' name, amen.

THE QUESTIONS

- Have you ever been sent by your local congregation to do something that carried the heart of your fellowship into an area of need?

- What gifts were a part of that experience for you?

THE HOLY SPIRIT IS A GUARANTEE THAT THE NEW CREATION IS ON THE WAY

2 CORINTHIANS 5:5

Now the one who has fashioned us for this very purpose is God, who has given us the Spirit as a deposit, guaranteeing what is to come.

If you had the opportunity today to know what the next ten years would hold, would you want to know? Many of us think we would be eager to know what is ahead, but that's usually only when we're thinking about the joys, the blessings, the good things, or even the bad things we would hope we could avoid.

But if the moment came, and I knew I would begin to expect what was to come in one, three, five, or seven years from now—I think I'd pass. A long season of anticipating a good thing is a delight; but a long season of anticipating the dark nights of the soul that lie ahead is quite another.

What about the future would I *want* to know? I would want to know where it's all going, so I could *hope*, and would find strength to persevere through whatever presented itself. I would want a promise of joy that would sustain me, even be alive within me, always whispering, encouraging me, and giving me the strength to go on.

That is exactly what the Father did in sending us the Holy Spirit. The Spirit is a deposit, a deep, divine, living promise, *guaranteeing* what is to come.

This is how hope works: assured of good ahead that we cannot see but can anticipate in our bones, the Spirit communicating to our spirit within, we then have the grace to bear the burdens we may face. The Holy Spirit in us, with us, and moving among us as a people is a sign, a first payment, communicating that the full reward is on the way. Paul used a word that was used in financial transactions of his time to note that through the Holy Spirit given to indwell the church, the Father has confirmed his promise that the rest of his goodness is *on the way*.

And what is on the way? Jesus inaugurated the kingdom of God, manifest among us and within the reach of every human being, pointing the way to the reality that there is a new creation ahead. Death is not the end. We will be resurrected from the dead, like our Lord before us. Our bodies will be raised, imperishable, whole and fit for the eternal delights ahead. Every tear will be wiped from your eyes and mine. There will be no more bad news. No more slave trafficking. No more hatred. No more wars. No more pandemics. No more division. No more cancer or lying or suicide or fear or *anything* that now runs against the shalom of Christ, the Prince of Peace, permeating the world.

When we experience the Holy Spirit—and the Spirit's gifts—we are experiencing none other than the promised Eden ahead, the New Jerusalem, the eternal dwelling of God among us, to come.

Forgiveness, powered by the Spirit, is an ensign reminding us sin and offense between us will one day disappear. Healing and kindness signal that this world is on its way to the next. When we minister to one another with love, joy, peace, patience, kindness, goodness, faithfulness, gentleness, and self-control, our capacity to do so in the face of adversity reminds us that the world will not end in destruction—it will end in a new creation flourishing!

Let the Holy Spirit, the *eschatological* Spirit,[10] stir your heart with worship as the Scriptures remind you of what is to come:

> Then I saw "a new heaven and a new earth," for the first heaven and the first earth had passed away, and there was no longer any sea. I saw the Holy City, the new Jerusalem, coming down out of heaven from God, prepared as a bride beautifully dressed for her husband. And I heard a loud voice from the throne saying, "Look! God's dwelling place is now among the people, and he will dwell with them. They will be his people, and God himself will be with them and be their God. 'He will wipe every tear from their eyes. There will be no more death' or mourning or crying or pain, for the old order of things has passed away."
>
> He who was seated on the throne said, "I am making everything new!" Then he said, "Write this down, for these words are trustworthy and true." (Rev. 21:1–5)

---

10. Gordon Fee, *Paul, the Spirit, and the People of God* (Grand Rapids: Baker Academic, 1996), ix.

THE PRAYER

Jesus, I receive the Holy Spirit. Lift my heart to sing the new song, the words of worship, that guide my spirit to the reality of the new creation ahead. Come, Holy Spirit, lead me to live in the way of Jesus; I want to be a sign that a new world is on the way. I pray in Jesus' name, amen.

THE QUESTIONS

- Have you ever felt, deep in your spirit, that the new creation to come was as real as the world you are living in now?

- What kind of environment were you in, and how did the Spirit encourage you?

THE HOLY SPIRIT HELPS US WAIT

GALATIANS 5:5

For through the Spirit we eagerly await by faith
the righteousness for which we hope.

Baking shows are a big hit these days. We love to see the creativity that kicks in when beautiful cakes, breads, and sandwiches are made that reveal the craft of baking has been mastered. In baking, you can't fake the bake. If the cake or bread was baked for the wrong amount of time, too short or too long, it just doesn't turn out right. You can't hurry the process, or extend it. The ingredients must be right—but the timing must also be just right.

It's been said that doing things right can provide a false sense that we are doing right things. Legalism can give us a sigh of relief when applied. But when the Holy Spirit comes, things don't always move quickly, nor do they always provide the immediate gratification we desire. If God is not acting, or is not acting in the way we desire, we can find and follow a rule, stoke the fires of religious service, and feel quite satisfied that we are doing something technically right—even without actually experiencing the presence of God. We are getting the bread without the flavor, texture, and end results that would serve everyone best.

And that's how religion can end up going wrong. Worship, spiritual activities, and disciplines can become ends in themselves, quick fixes that displace our need to wait on God when the good things he is always doing in the background are taking a smidge too long. King Saul did it when he had to wait for days for the prophet Samuel to arrive. When his army began to scatter, he did the thing that was technically "doing things right"—he offered a sacrifice. But it wasn't the right thing to do. The right thing to do was to *wait* for Samuel to offer the sacrifice (1 Sam. 13:5–13).

In Galatians 5, Paul is having an issue with the rigid religious streak that is running through a few of the followers of Jesus. They are in a hurry to get outward conformity by the group to Jewish religious practice. They will breathe a sigh of relief if they do. In verse 1, Paul tells them that freedom is the reason Christ came, not to lead us into deeper bondage to rules that provide quick gratification and keep everything under the rule of our spiritual timing. He also says, "Now the Lord is the Spirit, and where the Spirit of the Lord is, there is freedom" (2 Cor. 3:17). Quick fixes put us in greater bondage to rules that hold no power. The Spirit will not have it.

They were trying to find salvation by following rules, and demanding that others follow the same rules to keep the whole system in glorious check.

The body of Christ in every generation has suffered with *impatience*. We are in a spiritual *hurry*, and hurry has many manifestations. But we are not *in a hurry*; the *hurry is in us*. For all the seemingly right reasons, we pursue wrong goals—like filling seats and feeling good about our social media share counts without doing the deep work of one-on-one discipleship. The hurry is within us—and the Spirit will resist it by not letting our hurry, ultimately, prosper.

The false hope that doing religion can provide deceives us into thinking we're moving God's agenda along, when the agenda we have been moving along is actually our own. Paul comes to verse 7 in Galatians 5 saying: "You were running a good race. Who cut in on you to keep you from obeying the truth?" We must stay true to intimacy with God that is marked by the spiritual fruit of trust and *patience*. Without patience, we will be tripped up on the race and disqualified on our way to Christ. The Spirit will help us wait, with anticipation, for the final results that will come in God's perfect timing.

THE PRAYER

Jesus, I receive the Holy Spirit. The hurry in me must come to an end, lest I lean on my religious practices without actually investing myself in growing in spiritual intimacy with you. Come, Holy Spirit, I welcome you to slow my heart down, empowering me to wait on you to bring your best results—in your time. I pray in Jesus' name, amen.

THE QUESTIONS

- Can you identify with the idea that you are not in a hurry—the hurry is in you?

- What could you do to learn patience from the Holy Spirit?

THE HOLY SPIRIT GIVES US DIVINE PERSPECTIVE

PSALM 73:16–17

When I tried to understand all this, it troubled me deeply till
I entered the sanctuary of God; then I understood . . .

The only thing that people lose more than their keys or glasses is their *perspective*. Seeing our lives from the Father's vantage point is a deep, ongoing work of the Holy Spirit. And the process of seeing ourselves and everyone around us from God's perspective can be nurtured; we can partner with the Spirit in keeping a divine perspective winning in our lives.

The entire Bible resounds with this important announcement: *the work of awakening in the human heart can be long, slow, and incremental.* Psalm 73 is a psalm dedicated to documenting the process of a heart that has been awakened becoming awakened once again. In fact, it can read like an awakening movie plot playing itself out— hero is strong, hero is weak, hero overcomes old weakness revealed by new challenges, hero comes out stronger than before.

In the beginning our hero, a faithful yet wobbling believer, is struggling to remain firm in faith and hope. A low- or high-level despair has taken over, and the psalmist's words have been hijacked in the process. With an honest confession leading the way, the writer says, "But as for me, my feet had almost slipped; I had nearly lost my foothold. For I envied the arrogant when I saw the prosperity of the wicked" (Ps. 73:2–3). Let's bring this into our modern-day, post-Acts 2 reality.

In verses 4–14, the writer clarifies the conundrum: people who don't follow God have it better than those who do—why? They thrive; we suffer. God doesn't seem to mind this psalm spending quite a bit of time on the writer's deep wrestling, and nor should we. Honesty is a prerequisite to experiencing the fullness of the Spirit's presence, and unless we know and say what we're really battling with on the inside, we can never fully surrender the conundrum to Christ.

The writer is writing for us all, so we can personalize the pain in this psalm. We feel alone. We lose our way. We want to do the right things, but the things we hate we end up doing (Rom. 7:15). We envy. We wish. We prefer. We lust. We fear. We wonder, question, doubt, struggle, and sometimes find it offensive that we who choose the path of life seem to get the raw end of the deal when it comes to trouble.

Chaos-thinking can be distorting and oppressive. We begin to entertain errant thoughts that reinforce our worst fears—all this devotion has been for nothing; all of it is meaningless. And where is the Holy Spirit in all of that for the Christian? According to the Bible, the Spirit is in us, and with us, even as we spin our wheels in the mud of wailing and complaining for God's good and right to subvert the wrong that seems to be our daily portion. Into the chaos, into the brooding meaninglessness, the Spirit moves to bring order, to bring life, to bring light.

It is here that verses 16–17 unveil a powerful principle in our ongoing receiving of the Holy Spirit. "When I tried to understand all this, it troubled me deeply till I entered the sanctuary of God; then I understood." Our hero puts himself/herself *in the position* to encounter the Spirit by entering the sanctuary to experience the presence of God. Worship happens, and when it does, from the heart, it's like our head gets a spiritual shake: *What was I thinking?* we ask. Thank God for the Holy Spirit, who leads us to even consider our thinking might be off, askew, problematic.

Putting ourselves in the path of God's presence by entering the sanctuary of our daily meeting with God opens us up to the Spirit's perspective. It is in the place of worship that the Spirit helps our minds apprehend reality. Worship passionately and frequently as you walk with the Holy Spirit. In the midst of acclaiming God for his person, goodness, and love, you will find your perspective slowly changing to become the perspective of your Father in heaven.

THE PRAYER

Jesus, I receive the Holy Spirit. I know the power of envy, and how I can turn my focus to it quickly when I am in a time of challenge or fear. Come, Holy Spirit, let there be a fresh awakening in my heart this week as I enter into the sanctuaries given to me for the purpose of worship. Teach me to never withhold worship, especially in my times of greatest challenge. I pray in Jesus' name, amen.

THE QUESTION

- Can you remember a time you felt you had lost your perspective, only to find that clarity and trust returned when you drew near to God in worship?

THE HOLY SPIRIT OPENS US TO THE FATHER'S LOVE

GALATIANS 4:6

Because you are his sons, God sent the Spirit of his Son into
our hearts, the Spirit who calls out, "*Abba*, Father."

Recently I performed a wedding, in two languages, for my beautiful niece and her new husband. Hundreds of people attended, and the room was animated by family and friends from Mexico and across the United States. As a mariachi band played and the venue buzzed with conversation, my eyes scanned the crowd.

I saw many people I love and others I am coming to love. But I found myself scanning the room for a few particular people. These people were the ones I most wanted to look at, to smile at, and to know I was present with them.

I was looking for my children.

To see them dancing, laughing, talking, and glancing my way (on occasion) was the highlight of the gathering for me. My best thoughts are of their good, and my worst thoughts are of them being in pain—especially a pain that would distance us from one another. In fact, to bring the metaphor home, to imagine any of my children ever putting on a front to impress me, performing to secure my love, or forgetting how much I adore them is, to put it bluntly, sickening. But that is exactly what many Christians do when they live unawakened to the love of the Father.

We are sons and daughters, children of God in his great and marvelous world. But a dislocating pain is waiting to oust us from our identity as the Father's beloved every hour of every day that we live. Today the news will emphasize the darkness all around us, and because the brain craves warnings, and warnings equal more views, clicks, and shares, it will suck us in. Truth be told, today God's good world will remain disorienting at best, and destructive at worst. The enemy has free rein for a season; but then, there is the *Spirit*.

The Spirit reminds us that being a child of God means that we *belong* to Someone, that we are *cared for* by Someone. We are not alone in our hours or moments, nor are we to be afraid of being unaccepted, unappreciated, or unloved. But we will forget. We will forget we are accepted, appreciated, loved.

We will put on a false self to present to the world, and even those closest to us, so no one will see the disconsolate child crying within. As J. D. Walt says, "Growing in the grace of the gospel means a long process of emptying ourselves of all this falseness . . . that we might be filled with true fullness."[11] The fullness we seek is the Father's love. There is no supplanting its value and worth to the human heart. All wholeness is predicated upon it.

It's not until we stop performing, stop overcompensating, stop appearing to have it all together that we can even begin to see the state of our own hearts and to offer them to the Father. I have

---

11. J. D. Walt, "What to Do When Your Fullness Is Emptiness," Seedbed, April 21, 2021, https://www.seedbed.com/what-to-do-when-your-fullness -is-emptiness/.

awakened one day to the love of the Father overwhelming me, and the very next day I am back to my old habits of trying to impress others so they don't see how broken I really am.

The word for today is simple. The Spirit of Jesus, the beloved Son of God, is in our hearts. That Spirit within is settled, and from within us calls out to the Father, simultaneously reminding us, in the process, that we are his child. You are the beloved, the treasured, the prized, the delightful, the precious, the beautiful child of God. The Spirit reminds you of this truth at this moment, just as the Spirit is reminding me as well.

The Father's eyes are scanning the room with love—and he's looking for *you*.

THE PRAYER

Jesus, I receive the Holy Spirit. It is possible I may never fully comprehend your love for me, but I'd like to die trying. Come, Holy Spirit, keep my awareness high that I have no need to perform for you to love me more than you do right now. I pray in Jesus' name, amen.

THE QUESTION

- Share with others a moment in your life where you felt completely loved for who you are. How did that moment change your life, and how close are you to understanding that kind of love and acceptance that is flowing from the Father to you in this season of your life?

DAN WILT

THE HOLY SPIRIT IS OUR INNER ENERGY SOURCE

EPHESIANS 3:16–19

I pray that out of his glorious riches he may strengthen you with power through his Spirit in your inner being, so that Christ may dwell in your hearts through faith. And I pray that you, being rooted and established in love, may have power, together with all the Lord's holy people, to grasp how wide and long and high and deep is the love of Christ, and to know this love that surpasses knowledge— that you may be filled to the measure of all the fullness of God.

I grew up across the street from a small electrical generating station that was crucial to the powering of homes in our entire neighborhood. If it was struck by lightning (and it was on occasion), or some other catastrophe happened to shut it down, we would be without power for our heat, refrigeration, lights, and more. Every day I walked to school I would walk past that little station. It was always humming, always making a sound that said, "I'm working, and because I'm working, so is your toaster."

Power is needed for living; we all know it. So how can we best get the personal power we need in a way that doesn't shoot us in the foot in the long run? Every day, people are experimenting with different kinds of personal power sources, and idols innumerable are offering their energy-generating potential at discount prices.

When we do find our personal, portable power source in Christ, the spiritually cleanest and most efficient energy source a soul can find (we were made for it, by design), there are energy-thieves at every turn seeking to steal or choke off what the Spirit provides.

In this passage in Ephesians, as in other passages, Paul is connecting the coming of power to our inner being to the presence of the Holy Spirit dwelling within. What is it, specifically, that Paul thinks we need power for?

First, we need power so that "Christ may dwell in" our "hearts through faith." Faith is a state of being where we are putting our highest hopes in a God we cannot see. When we walk in forgiveness, compassion, wisdom, understanding, love, joy, peace, patience, kindness, goodness, and self-control, it is like we are lighting up with the energy source of the Holy Spirit for living. When we walk in shades of the power-stealing ways of unforgiveness, a lack of mercy, ignorance, hatred, despair, unrest, impatience, unkindness, self-absorption, or lack of self-control, it's like we are draining our energy and the lights begin to flicker. Faith takes power, and yet power generates power when we trust Jesus as the indwelling energizer of our soul.

Second, we need power "to grasp how wide and long and high and deep is the love of Christ" and we need power "to know this love that surpasses knowledge." Comprehending our belovedness and the belovedness of others, Paul is saying, takes something beyond ourselves. The Spirit gives us the capability, the resource we need, to perceive God's love and to revel in it. The more we revel in the love God has for us, the more we light up with the energy source of the Holy Spirit for living. When we forget the fullness of Jesus' love for us, we flicker and, in some cases, flame out entirely.

The work of awakening begins in us, and we will need power to change, and power to become like Jesus in this world. According to this passage, the Spirit empowering our faith, and our awareness of love, is the key to moving ahead.

We are in discipleship training all along the way. Virtue takes an inner Olympian training, and the Spirit of Jesus is our coach. We are being energized to experience change and love, in order that we might become agents of change and love in the world. The latter follows the former. We are being changed to change, loved to love.

THE PRAYER

Jesus, I receive the Holy Spirit. If I am drawing on other personal power sources that are cutting me off from your best provision, reveal these to me so I can repent and turn again to you as my source. Come, Holy Spirit, give me power today to live in faith and in full awareness of your love—for myself and for those around me. I pray in Jesus' name, amen.

THE QUESTION

- What kind of spiritual energy do you need right now, and where are you finding it?

THE HOLY SPIRIT IS INVITING YOU TO PARTNER IN THE HEALING OF THE WORLD

JOHN 16:7

"But very truly I tell you, it is for your good that I am going away. Unless I go away, the Advocate will not come to you; but if I go, I will send him to you."

We're on holy ground when we are listening to the words of Jesus. When he spoke, he was not afraid of leading his disciples into a state of holy tension, where they were psychologically caught in-between two seemingly contradictory truths. In his words about the Holy Spirit being the Advocate, there is a tension that is created that we cannot deny—life is hard, yet the Holy Spirit is in us.

I regularly experience the feeling that I can do little to fix the great evils, injustices, and heartaches that are occurring in the world. I lament. I groan in intercessory prayer. I long for the Spirit to break the news cycle. I know the Holy Spirit is within me, and that I have a part to play, but the world remains overwhelming and exceedingly difficult to deal with. Rarely do the people or things I pray for change on a dime. My own awakening to love is ever-challenged, and I must fight the good fight for my own soul as well as others. I get tired. Worn out. Carried to the edges of my faith by waves I cannot seem to still like my Lord. That is one thing that is true.

Here is another thing that is true. In contrast to my feelings of powerlessness, the Holy Spirit says, "I can do something—and we can do something together." God's power is present to change people and situations, especially when one of us yields to the Spirit's leading. There is great pain that has been alleviated (think "hospitals"), even cut off at its source (think "abolition") because faithful people, empowered by the Holy Spirit, showed up and believed they could do something in partnership with God.

By faith in the Son of God they took up a vocation that came to them from another and worked through them for others—and they changed one tiny corner of the world with Christ. I can't deny it's true. None of us can. It's happened with me, and it's happened with you. The Holy Spirit is our Advocate, and through us, advocates (helps) others. That is another thing that is true.

We live in between the times of Christ's first and second coming. Christ's followers have had to live in the tension between the now and the not-yet of the kingdom of God for millennia. Like Peter, I often think, "Though you have not seen him, you love him; and even though you do not see him now, you believe in him and are filled with an inexpressible and glorious joy" (1 Peter 1:8). And yet, at the same time, Jesus' words in John 16:33 remain: "I have told you these things, so that in me you may have peace. In this world you will have trouble. But take heart! I have overcome the world."

Joy and trouble. A taste of God's love and a taste of death's sting. One will last forever, and the other is as temporary as anything could ever be. But still, we work toward, and long for, the new creation. We pray for, act for, and live for the world to be ruled by the Prince of Shalom, his peace and love permeating all things.

And as we wait, the Advocate lives and works within us. Our sanctification, our transformation into Christ-likeness, hinges only on us saying yes to joining the Holy Spirit in helping those around us. The rest, in the midst of our troubles, is up to him.

THE PRAYER

Jesus, I receive the Holy Spirit. There is a part I have to play with you as an advocate and a helper, becoming Jesus to my network of relationships. Come, Holy Spirit, show me the next place in which you are working, and show me how I can partner with you in that work today. I pray in Jesus' name, amen.

THE QUESTIONS

- Is there an invitation from the Holy Spirit, to be a helper, that you are aware of today?

- How will you respond?

THE SWORD OF THE SPIRIT IS THE WORD OF GOD

EPHESIANS 6:17

Take the helmet of salvation and the sword of
the Spirit, which is the word of God.

According to the Bible, there's a time to be gracious, peace-loving, kind, and even accommodating. According to the Bible, there is also a time to drop your gloves, to stop playing nice, and to fight with everything that is in you—dressed in spiritual armor to the nines (Eph. 6:10–18).

That time to fight with all you've got is in the spiritual battle for your soul. The key to winning that battle is to have the right battle in focus, and to have the right enemy in clear view. "For our struggle is not against flesh and blood, but against the rulers, against the authorities, against the powers of this dark world and against the spiritual forces of evil in the heavenly realms" (Eph. 6:12).

When it comes to the spiritual battle we find ourselves in, every day of every moment of our lives, any accommodation of the devil's aggressions will cause us to wind up another casualty on the battlefield of the heart. Satan's end is to destroy you, and like a roaring lion (1 Peter 5:8), devouring your precious life is the only task on his agenda today. The same goes for everyone else around you. Sleeping people don't fight for their lives. Only awakened people fight for their lives, and fight for others in prayer and loving action as well.

Yes, Virginia, there is a *spiritual war going on out there*. Worse yet, that *spiritual war is also going on in here*—in your heart, my heart, your mind, my mind, your body, and my body. All that God gives and means for good, for joy, and flourishing in your life, the enemy of our souls is relentlessly working to drag toward chaos. There's no neutral ground. We either believe in an enemy or we don't. We're either alert to his schemes or we aren't. We're either winning or we're losing, every single day.

The Spirit wants us to win; and gives us the weapon of the Word of God—the fullness of the gospel of our Lord Jesus Christ, the gift of the Scriptures, and the Spirit speaking to us—in order to do it.

Let's drive home the point so we don't miss it, and we aren't deluded. People are falling, left and right, every day, in a thousand small ways. People who think the world is fine as it is are, to be candid, the walking blind—people are dying every day from a lack of love and from believing satanic, demonic, destructive *lies*.

They fall bit by bit until one day they pass on, asleep to God in their spirits, lulled into a hypnotic trance by disordered desires and self-absorbed patterns. Some people even take their own life to escape the struggle. Others anesthetize their pain with myriad addictions and broken personality patterns. Most just hope bad things don't happen, and good things do. They are asleep to the battle raging within and around them.

What can cut through the mesmerizing sound hell's pied piper is playing to the world?

The sword of the Spirit can cut through, that's what. The Word of God. Living and active, it's "Sharper than any double-edged sword, it penetrates even to dividing soul and spirit, joints and marrow; it judges the thoughts and attitudes of the heart" (Heb. 4:12). Jesus confronted every one of the Accuser's temptations in the desert with the Word of God.

The church is given this same offensive weapon (notice that most of the others in Ephesians 6:10–18 are defensive weapons?). We were designed to wield the sword of the Spirit, the Word of God. Preach the Word of God, hide the Scriptures in your heart, and obey what the Spirit speaks to you in the moments he does. Share the gospel, and be ready to do offer its hope at any moment. Sing the Word of God. Teach the Word of God. Write and offer and share the Word of God.

It is the sword of the Spirit—for such a time as this.

THE PRAYER

Jesus, I receive the Holy Spirit. Your Word has come to us through the Scriptures and the mystery of the gospel. Come, Holy Spirit, teach me to wield it well in the day ahead, and to take my stand against the enemy's schemes (Eph. 6:11). I pray in Jesus' name, amen.

THE QUESTION

- Take a few moments to read about the armor of God, and the spiritual battle we are in, in Ephesians 6:10–18. How can you take up the sword of the Spirit for today's offensive mission (1 John 3:8)?

DAY 66

THE HOLY SPIRIT LEADS US INTO AWAKENING WORSHIP

JOHN 4:23-24

"Yet a time is coming and has now come when the true worshipers will worship the Father in the Spirit and in truth, for they are the kind of worshipers the Father seeks. God is spirit, and his worshipers must worship in the Spirit and in truth."

Have you ever walked into a room where worship music was being played and sung, your heart heavy and burdened, and in the space of singing one song you felt like your burdens had lifted? The Holy Spirit was working through the seen and unseen dynamics of worship. In worship, the truthful heart, your heart, opening to the Holy Spirit—is *reawakened*.

In John 4 (read at your leisure), as soon as Jesus speaks prophetically into a wayward woman's life, in her awe and amazement she thinks of the most important question she could ask such a person. Pause here with me. What a heart! She chooses to ask Jesus about worship! This pained woman was eager to get worship right—she wanted to know the how of worship, what pleases God, and who is right about how worship works. The questions in her heart could be rendered for us today:

- How should we worship Jesus?

- What songs should we use?

- Which prayers are the right prayers?

- How do we get the Holy Spirit to move in worship?

Do those questions matter? Absolutely. The Spirit moves in and through the details, and worship is discipleship—full stop. However, Jesus sidesteps her question about the best location to worship, and speaks to the question *behind* her question. She was asking a version of Psalm 42:2 in her spirit, and Jesus knew it: "My soul thirsts for God, for the living God. When can I go and meet with God?" Or, in this case, *where* can I go and meet with God?

Jesus' answer is beautiful: "A time is coming and has now come when the true worshipers will worship the Father in the Spirit and in truth, for they are the kind of worshipers the Father seeks. God is spirit, and his worshipers must worship in the Spirit and in truth" (John 4:23–24).

Jesus pointed the woman toward the who of worship, and put the how aside for the good of her soul. Jesus was locating the temple of worship in her *heart*. She didn't see that truth coming; her tradition, and the tradition of others, had taught her that the location, the mechanics, the rituals, the patterns of worship mattered most. Jesus, as he so masterfully does, presented a completely new (yet ancient) paradigm to her: "The LORD looks on the heart" (1 Sam. 16:7). The Spirit is always, always, about the heart. And so is worship.

When we come to worship with our honesty, our truthfulness, and our orientation to Christ and all he is, then truth is in the picture. We say to the Spirit within us, "Open my heart to worship you God, as you know yourself to be." Then, when worship, Spirit, and truth all mingle together, our soul opens to the life-changing power of God.

Come to every opportunity to worship, be it corporate or personal, with transparency and an orientation toward truth. Open yourself to be led by the Holy Spirit into worship. Then, expect to meet God in that holy place of adoration—your heart.

THE PRAYER

Jesus, I receive the Holy Spirit. Worship is a place of meeting with you, and the best location for that meeting is my heart; I am eager to be as present to you as I can possibly be. Come, Holy Spirit, lead me in worship as I do my part of orienting my heart to your truth and bringing with me my honesty to that place of meeting. I pray in Jesus' name, amen.

THE QUESTIONS

- Have you ever entered into a time of worship and found that your perspective was changed in the experience?

- What was it like?

DAN WILT

LIVING IN THE RIGHTEOUSNESS, PEACE, AND JOY OF THE HOLY SPIRIT

ROMANS 14:17–18

For the kingdom of God is not a matter of eating and drinking, but of righteousness, peace and joy in the Holy Spirit, because anyone who serves Christ in this way is pleasing to God and receives human approval.

Many of us have had the experience of standing in line at an airport, waiting to board a plane. My favorite moment is when the person over the loud speaker says, "We're now boarding families with children."

The parents, with relief in their eyes, begin to come forward. Nobody faults anyone else for letting the families go first. I don't see fellow passengers asking to see the family's boarding passes. The children are either sweetly smiling, tucked close to a parent's chest, wandering to the full arm's length of a distressed parent, or wailing in practice for the long performance ahead.

Sometimes the things we think are the most important, like us getting a seat in sync with our boarding pass number, can get in the way of a higher priority—making sure the families among us are settled and at peace first. We all benefit in the end, but our sense of propriety, fairness, and even justice may kick in and distort our ability to see the higher value right in front of us.

In Romans 14:17–18 we are being reminded of an important truth—quibbling about important things can get in the way of celebrating—and proliferating—the *more* important things.

For example, issues of "eating and drinking" were important to the Jews. In Romans 14:1–16, it seems there were many matters that were taking up the community's time and attention. In a culture where every liturgical action represented a spiritual truth (like eating and drinking the *agape* feast together), it was easy to prioritize the little details of worship and community practice based on the idea that "God cares about the details."

God cares about your boarding pass number. He cares that you booked early so you could get a good place in line. Well done. But sometimes, a *more* important value, a higher ideal, steps in and assigns other practices a different place in line. Sometimes, the families need to go *first*. To put it in the context of today's passage—sometimes the weaker one should be honored.

In fact, could it be that we let the little details get in the way because they are easier to find success in achieving, easier than acts that involve loving others more highly than ourselves, acting self-sacrificially toward someone who has a different take on a spiritual practice than you do, or laying down our lives for our brothers and sisters? Often the harder work we're avoiding is hidden behind our fixation on extra details and doing things right.

The Spirit won't let us off the hook—the Spirit will keep the main things the main things if we will listen and respond.

The Holy Spirit is at work in the body in Christ. Our integrity (righteousness), our peace-making (peace), and our steady and delighted rejoicing in the miracle of God's love being at work in our hearts and in the right-side-upping of the world (joy) are of highest importance.

The Holy Spirit is forming the church to be Christlike on the inside, and Christlike on the outside. The kingdom Jesus came to inaugurate is all about opening the heart to the Father's love—starting with righteousness, peace, and joy, sparked by the kingdom actions of walking with one another in integrity, doing the work of peace-making among us, and rejoicing in the Lord always—these are the priorities the Spirit keeps ever before us.

The Spirit of Jesus knows what, and who, should go first in line. Let's allow the Spirit to shuffle what we think of being our highest values, so the Spirit can show us what the Father values most.

THE PRAYER

Jesus, I receive the Holy Spirit. It is sometimes easier to focus on details that matter, but don't matter as much as other things, because the other, the more important and lasting things of the heart, are harder to do. Come, Holy Spirit, realign what I prioritize and value so I can live out your dreams in the world you so love. I pray in Jesus' name, amen.

THE QUESTIONS

- Are there any details about your faith or walk with God that you've allowed to displace the harder things into which he's inviting you?

- What are they, and how could you realign your values to match the higher values of the heart of which the Spirit is reminding you?

THE HOLY SPIRIT FILLS THE TEMPLE OF THE CHURCH

1 CORINTHIANS 3:16

Don't you know that you yourselves are God's temple
and that God's Spirit dwells in your midst?

Friend, intercessor, Spirit-filled child of God, and ambassador of awakening—we have something to do with Jesus in the world today, just as our family across the ages had something to do in their day, their time, their such-a-moment-as-this visitation of the Spirit.

We, the family of Christ, the temple of the Holy Spirit, the body of Jesus Christ, are a spiritual household of living stones being built together (1 Peter 2:4–6). You and I each have a part to play in what the Father is doing in our day—without you, without each of us doing our part, we are lesser. With you, and the Spirit-life you are living, we are richer!

From the beginning of time until now, the Holy Spirit has been meeting the demonic spirit of chaos in the world, head on, with God's good and loving *order*. The Holy Spirit has been confronting the spirit of meaninglessness, in all its packages and forms and with all its hideous results, with *meaningfulness*.

And that is our job as well. As the temple of the Holy Spirit, we do what Jesus did, his Spirit growing in us the fruits of the Spirit, empowering us with the gifts of the Spirit, and teaching us to walk according to the Story of the Spirit. We move in the world, Spirit-renewed and self-renewed in our sense of purpose, joy, mission, and hope.

The Holy Spirit has always used believing, trusting, and worshiping people to accomplish his purposes. We travail in prayer. We act in unparalleled mercy. We suffer with uncommon grace. We worship with living hope. We show the world what Jesus looks like—giving, loving, serving, encouraging, challenging, and living just as he did. We who seek to live faithfully to Jesus are a community through which his Spirit moves—whether we are all together in one place or spread out across the globe (or across the ages)!

And now for a Kingdom Public Service Announcement: The gates of hell *have not prevailed against the church*. They never will (Matt. 16:17–19)! Awakened people beget awakened people. Your work and mine is to stay present to the love, presence, and will of the Father as we pass on the truly good life to those in our sphere of influence. There is no higher call. The Spirit fills the church, his temple, to this end.

Remember when the Spirit filled Solomon's temple with the glory of God in 2 Chronicles 7? Here is Solomon's prayer that preceded that glorious encounter:

> "But will God really dwell on earth with humans? The heavens, even the highest heavens, cannot contain you. How much less this temple I have built! Yet, LORD my God, give attention to your servant's prayer and his plea for mercy. Hear the cry and the prayer that your servant is praying in your presence. *May your eyes be*

open toward this temple day and night, this place of which you said you would put your Name there. May you hear the prayer your servant prays toward this place." (2 Chron. 6:18–20, emphasis added)

"May your eyes be open toward this temple day and night." The Father's eyes are on his temple, his church. They are on *you*, just as they are on *us*. We are the cared for, watched over, loved-beyond-measure, and the filled-and-empowered body of Christ. When the going gets tough, is when the temple of the Holy Spirit gets going. Now is the time, again, for us to show up with Christlikeness on the terrain of our homes, churches, cities, and nations. You are not alone in revealing Christ. You never were. We receive you, Holy Spirit—fill your temple once again!

THE PRAYER

Jesus, we receive the Holy Spirit. As your temple, your church, we say yes to praying without ceasing, being your hands and feet in the world, and loving with the kind of love that can only come from heaven. Come, Holy Spirit, we are ready to play our part in our generation, once again. I pray in Jesus' name, amen.

THE QUESTIONS

- What stories from church history inspire you about the way the church acted in a time of great challenge?

- How does that story encourage you about our role today?

THE HOLY SPIRIT HELPS US IN OUR WEAKNESS

ROMANS 8:26–27

In the same way, the Spirit helps us in our weakness. We do not know what we ought to pray for, but the Spirit himself intercedes for us through wordless groans. And he who searches our hearts knows the mind of the Spirit, because the Spirit intercedes for God's people in accordance with the will of God.

Have you felt weak lately, falling behind as you chase the "Mighty Child of God" success wagon down the street? Or are you generally fearful as you consider if your own spiritual life can withstand the test of your current trials—and the test of time?

We can be grateful today that Jesus understood weakness, suffering, and pain. We can also take great peace from the fact that the Holy Spirit, living within us, is familiar with the kinds of pain we endure. Everyone else may not know what you are carrying today—but your Father knows.

Isaiah, prophesying of the "suffering servant" said: "He was despised and rejected by mankind, a man of suffering, and familiar with pain. . . . Surely he took up our pain and bore our suffering . . . he was pierced for our transgressions, he was crushed for our iniquities; the punishment that brought us peace was on him, and by his wounds we are healed" (Isa. 53:3–5, selections).

"By his wounds, we are healed." Weakness happens. Suffering happens. Pain happens. And yet—and yet—as Romans 8:9a reminds us: "You, however, are not in the realm of the flesh but are in the realm of the Spirit, if indeed the Spirit of God lives in you." The Spirit is at work, within us, healing our wounds, empowering our recoveries, and strengthening us in the midst of enduring pain. It's true. We must own it, and believe it. However, you are being healed and helped in this season of your life, you can trust the Spirit is at work in it all.

There are many great insights being offered out there in the world today for how to better care for ourselves and others. Our spiritual health, our mental health, our emotional health, and our physical health all flow together to determine our overall health as a human being. We can draw from the good, and reject the unhelpful, as we follow Jesus.

But no matter how many insights come from the "buy our product/plan/book, and your wounds will be healed" world around us, even generously offered from skilled practitioners and wise people, there is no greater strength that anyone can have for overcoming weakness than *the Holy Spirit living within us*. "The Spirit helps us in our weakness" (Rom. 8:26). Paul wrote: "I consider that our present sufferings are not worth comparing with the glory that will be revealed in us" (Rom. 8:18).

Your sufferings, my sufferings, are offset by the hope of new creation that is before us. All things will be made new. We will rise from death whole, complete, and without sickness or pain. We will see the healing and wholeness of things we so long to see in this lifetime.

There is a glory that will be revealed in you. Take a deep breath, and trust Jesus, again, today. The Spirit will help you in your weakness.

Jesus, I receive the Holy Spirit. I surrender my weakness to you, knowing that only you can convert it to a spiritual strength that makes me resilient for a lifetime. Come, Holy Spirit, give me faith for my healing, and faith for enduring; I welcome both from your presence within me. I pray in Jesus' name, amen.

THE QUESTIONS

- What weakness are you most challenged by right now?

- How is the Spirit helping you to overcome it?

A BRIEF HISTORY OF THE HOLY SPIRIT IN THE SCRIPTURES

REVELATION 22:17

The Spirit and the bride say, "Come!" And let the one who hears say, "Come!" Let the one who is thirsty come; and let the one who wishes take the free gift of the water of life.

We're coming to the conclusion of our journey through the Scriptures, exploring the person and work of the Holy Spirit. Like looking at a photo album after a wonderful trip, let's take a few moments to worshipfully view all the places we've been.

Today, awareness of the activity of the Holy Spirit is as vital to the church as it has ever been. The Spirit invites us to an infilling, a deep drink, of the living water Jesus offers us.

Jesus said to his disciples, "Receive the Holy Spirit" in John 20:21–22. As we open ourselves to the Holy Spirit today, there will be parties of salvation and joy (Acts 2:1), a few things will get moved around (Acts 2:2), we'll be filled with the fire of love for others (Acts 2:3), and we'll be empowered with gifts for the mission of loving the world to life in Jesus' name (Acts 2:4–8, 11b).

We learn from the Old Testament (the Hebrew Bible), that the Holy Spirit is the Breath of God (*ruakh*) and the Original Artist (Gen. 1:1), bringing beauty from chaos (Gen. 1:2), animating human life (Gen. 2:7), and sustaining all things seen and unseen (Gen. 2:1). The Holy Spirit speaks to people (Gen. 15:12a), helps us obey (Gen. 22:1–2), rushes to a humble heart (1 Sam. 16:13a), and renews us in worship (Ps. 51:10–12).

The Holy Spirit is with us everywhere (Ps. 139:7–10), leading us to the good life (Ps. 143:10), stirring praise in our spirit (Ex. 15:19–21), and welcoming us to awakening moments (Ex. 3:2–4). The Spirit gives us prophetic discernment (Gen. 41:38), works through our skills (Ex. 31:1–6), orchestrates such-a-time-as-this moments (Esther 4:12–14), and uses God-hearing leaders (Judges 4:14). The Spirit gives us a heart of flesh (Ezek. 36:26–27), calls a kingdom of priests (Ex. 19:4–6a), pours out God's presence (Joel 2:28–29; 32a), and rests on the Messiah (Isa. 11:1–3). The Holy Spirit empowers the good news that sets captives free (Isa. 61:1–2a), and gives us life (Job 33:4).

We learn from the New Testament that Jesus was with the wind (*pneuma*) of the Holy Spirit at creation (John 1:1–5), and the Spirit gives us the strength to obey (Luke 1:35)— working powerfully through a person aware of the Father's love (Matt. 3:16–17). The Spirit makes us born again (John 3:5–8), is our Helper (John 14:16–17), reveals Jesus (John 15:26), and guides us into all truth (John 16:13). The Spirit glorifies Jesus (John 16:14–15; 17:23) and reveals to us the depths of God (1 Cor. 2:9–10). The Spirit always builds up the body of Christ (1 Cor. 12:12–14), empowers us with the Father's love (Rom. 8:14–15), and teaches us what to say when we need to declare our faith (Luke 12:11–12). By the Spirit we learn how to walk on the path of life (Gal. 5:16–18), experience freedom

3:17), gain the fruitful character of Christ (Gal. 5:22–23), ₍h our spiritual thirst (John 7:37–39), and come out of ₍rts with power (Luke 4:1–2, 14–15).

₍he Holy Spirit is the Spirit of Jesus' resurrection within us (Rom. 8:11), lavishly given by the Father (Luke 11:13), showing us the way of love (1 Cor. 13:1–7), and equipping us for ministry with profound spiritual gifts (1 Cor. 12:1–2). That great symphony of spiritual gifts (1 Cor. 12:7) is expressed through the church, and gifts are distributed to all (1 Cor. 12:4–6), many and abundant (1 Cor. 12:8–11), for the building up of the local church (Rom. 12:4–8).

The Holy Spirit strengthens the body through gifted leaders (Eph. 4:11–13), speaks to us through the Scriptures (2 Tim. 3:14–17), through impressions and intuitions (Acts 20:22–24), through gifts of wisdom (James 3:13, 17; Col. 1:9–12), and through the body of Christ (Acts 13:2–3; Rom. 12:5). The Spirit is a deposit and guarantee of resurrection and the new creation to come (2 Cor. 5:5), helping us wait in hope (Gal. 5:5), giving us divine perspective (Ps. 73:16–17), and opening us to the Father's love (Gal. 4:6).

We are strengthened inwardly by the Spirit (Eph. 3:16–19), and invited to partner in the healing of the world (John 16:7). The sword of the Spirit is God's Word (Eph. 6:17) and worship is to flow from us in Spirit and in truth (John 4:23–24). The Holy Spirit gives us righteousness, peace, and joy (Rom. 14:17–18), fills the temple of the church (1 Cor. 3:16), and helps us in our weakness (Rom. 8:26–27). And the Holy Spirit does much, much more.

While experiences with the Holy Spirit can't be manufactured, they can be nurtured. Breathe deeply of the Holy Spirit, and drink deeply of the living waters Jesus promised. The church of

Jesus Christ is given the gift of the Holy Spirit—for the sake of the world.

Receive the Holy Spirit!

THE PRAYER

Jesus, I receive the Holy Spirit! My heart is full just reading about your work in history and your work in us as your church. Come, Holy Spirit, I receive you with my whole heart; fill me with your presence. I pray in Jesus' name, amen.

THE QUESTIONS

- Are you ready to be a part of the history of the Holy Spirit in our day and time?

- What is the next step you could take to do this?

ACKNOWLEDGMENTS

It is only appropriate that I acknowledge my deep debt to New Testament scholar Gordon Fee for his important work helping the body of Christ reclaim our rich inheritance—the Spirit of God at work in and through the church. Fee's book, *Paul, the Spirit, and the People of God*, had a tremendous impact on me when I first read it, and his work continues to shape my thinking and feeling as a disciple as I daily learn what it means to live according to the Spirit (Rom. 8:5).

It is also appropriate for me to thank the Vineyard Movement, my immediate family within the body of Christ, and my mentors throughout the years, who showed me what a life guided by the Holy Spirit could look like. The thousands of naturally supernatural stories of miracles, of encounters with the presence of God in worship, and of transformation by the Spirit's power have formed me both by hearing and participation. I will never look back, and I will never be the same.

I would like to thank my friends and co-laborers at Seedbed. You pursue God's best, cheer one another on, and seek the fullness of God's kingdom being expressed among us. It's a privilege to serve together—toward the awakening of a generation. Thank you.

Finally, I would like to thank my wife, Anita, and my children for being signs of the Holy Spirit's work at every turn. I am grateful to share the journey together.

9 781628 2492